D I Y
Stamped Metal Jewelry

D I Y
Stamped Metal Jewelry

From Monogrammed Pendants to Embossed Bracelets—
30 Easy Jewelry Pieces from HappyHourProjects.com!

Adrianne Surian

Avon, Massachusetts

Published by
Adams Media, a division of F+W Media, Inc.
57 Littlefield Street, Avon, MA 02322. U.S.A.
www.adamsmedia.com

ISBN 10: 1-4405-9666-2
ISBN 13: 978-1-4405-9666-7
eISBN 10: 1-4405-9667-0
eISBN 13: 978-1-4405-9667-4

Printed in the United States of America.

10 9 8 7 6 5 4 3 2 1

Library of Congress Cataloging-in-Publication Data

Surian, Adrianne, author.
DIY stamped metal jewelry / Adrianne Surian.
Avon, Massachusetts: Adams Media, 2016.
Includes index.
LCCN 2016015155 (print) | LCCN 2016023074 (ebook) | ISBN
  9781440596667 (pb) | ISBN 1440596662 (pb) | ISBN 9781440596674 (ebook)
  | ISBN 1440596670 (ebook)
LCSH: Jewelry making. | Metal stamping. | BISAC: CRAFTS & HOBBIES /
  Jewelry. | CRAFTS & HOBBIES / Metal Work. | CRAFTS & HOBBIES / Fashion.
LCC TT212 .S88 2016 (print) | LCC TT212 (ebook) | DDC 745.594/2--dc23
LC record available at https://lccn.loc.gov/2016015155

Cover design by Frank Rivera.
Cover images by Adrianne Surian.
Interior art by Adrianne Surian.

This book is available at quantity discounts for bulk purchases.
For information, please call 1-800-289-0963.

dedication

For Raya and Roman, who inherited my love of hammers;
for Kevin, who gives me tools instead of flowers;
and for friends near and far who have encouraged me to do great things.

You are my inspiration.

contents

introduction

DIY Stamped Metal Jewelry will teach you everything you need to know about stamping metal, from your first piece to exploring a whole world of fabulous, creative techniques! Jewelry-making is as much an art form as it is a science; as you complete these projects—like the Adventurer's Double-Pendant Necklace (see Chapter 3) or the Fearless Leather Cuff (see Chapter 4)—you will find ways to express yourself that are entirely your own. How awesome! This book is meant to get you started stamping quickly and confidently. All of your pieces, from your first tries to your experienced creations, will look fabulous!

I started stamping metal jewelry in 2011. At that time, it was difficult to find supplies, and even harder to find anyone who would share techniques for free. Classes were expensive, and personalized stamped metal jewelry was a hot seller online. I was determined to learn it, though, so for my birthday I overpaid for a beginner stamping set, and then spent hours doing a terrible job. But I'm stubborn, so as I kept at it, I learned a lot along the way! I've also picked up a few tips from professionals in the industry, and in the end, I discovered my favorite ways to create beautiful pieces of jewelry and more with my hammer and stamps. I continue to find innovative ways to use stamping to create works of jewelry art. I share my adventures in the world of metal stamping on my blog, HappyHourProjects.com, to teach others who are interested in stamping—without all the hassle I went through to learn.

Here you'll find out everything you need to know to start stamping your own gorgeous, personalized jewelry. Start with Chapter 1 to discover what tools and materials you'll need—as well as my best tips for when to save, when to splurge, and where to find everything. In Chapter 2 you'll find all of the techniques you will need to make every project in this book: from stamping letters to creating patterns to using patinas to create a custom look. From there, you'll be ready to roll on any stamping project that strikes your fancy, or even ones you dream up.

As you work through the projects, you'll find earrings for a girls' night out, necklaces that show your funny side, and bracelets you can wear for every occasion. Stamped jewelry fits every wardrobe and every style, because it's an expression of you! There are 30 designs in this book to inspire you when you make your next accessory or your next gift, ranging from classic to trendy and from sweet to sassy. Stamped metal jewelry is so much more than just the classic initials necklace.

Throughout, you'll see extra tips, tricks, and ideas under the hashtags #stampinghacks and #happystamping. These hashtags are used by the awesome HappyHourProjects.com community across all social media platforms to share our projects and encourage one another! Under #stampinghacks, I'll point out some tricks of the trade to help you easily learn fun new techniques. #happystamping will give you plenty of variation ideas to make these projects truly your own. Remember to use these hashtags to share your creations with the stamping community—we cannot wait to see what you create, so let's get stamping!

CHAPTER 1

Tools and Materials

Metal stamping is the practice of using a small hammer tool to gently tap a stamp (a small, solid rod of metal that has a raised design or letter at one end) onto a metal surface, called a metal blank, to create an impression. These impressions are your patterns, monograms, shapes, and words that you can use to make jewelry to express yourself and wear what you love.

Stamps are available in nearly every style you can imagine, from whimsical designs and script letters to bold and modern choices, with new options available all the time. You can create beautiful accessories with basic tools and supplies, but as with so many areas of crafts and design, there's also plenty of room to grow and expand your collection once you find that you have a real passion for personalizing metal jewelry.

Here you'll learn about the basic tools and materials needed to create your very own stamped metal jewelry and to get great results right from the start.

TOOLS

There are tools specifically made for metal stamping. These tools will enable you to create everything from metal cuff bracelets to beaded earrings, and beyond. Metal-stamping tools and supplies are finally making their way into craft stores as this hobby increases in popularity, so if you have a major arts and crafts retailer near you, all you need is a trip to the store to find everything you need to get started. If you don't have a major outlet nearby, try inquiring at a local bead shop, or source your supplies online. Prices vary quite a bit, even for the same tools, so comparison shopping can save you quite a bit of money. You should be able to get your starter supplies for around U.S. $100.

Steel Blocks (or Steel Bench Blocks)

The first tool you need in order to get a great result when stamping is a steel block (or steel bench block) for a work surface that will both give you a crisp impression and protect your work table. You can't skip the steel block if you want to stamp! It's a critical tool. Steel blocks are simple slabs of hardened steel, often square, and can be quite heavy the larger they are.

Steel blocks are much like the desk in your office; they come in different sizes with different features for your comfort. If you stamp a great deal—or think you will—invest in an extra-large steel block at 6" square. This is the size you will see used throughout the book. If you want to try out stamping before splurging on a large block, there are blocks

as small as 1½" square. Some blocks come with rubberized bottoms to absorb noise. As with a desk, you can pay extra for certain features, but in truth, you can get the same quality of work done no matter which block you choose.

Hammers

When choosing hammers, you have many options, each with a specific purpose and use. Depending on your personal style, you may find that you use many hammers regularly, or that a good brass hammer is all you need. Each of the following hammers has a special purpose in your stamper's toolset.

Brass Hammer

The typical stamping hammer is a one-pound brass hammer with a shortened handle. The brass helps absorb some of the shock so that your hands don't ache at the end of a long stamping session, and the shortened handle of the stamping hammer gives you much more control than a standard hammer. While I highly recommend a one-pound brass stamping hammer, I'll be perfectly honest: I began stamping with the one-pound hammer that I found in my household tool box. Working with a small standard hammer is just fine if you're starting out and want to save some money, but as soon as you decide you're a stamper at heart, it'll be the very first piece you will want to upgrade.

Nylon Hammer

A nylon hammer is a good tool to invest in, because you may find on occasion that thin metal blanks—the small pieces of metal you are stamping into—can bow slightly as you stamp them. The nylon hammer will allow you to flatten out these blanks without marring the metal. Nylon hammers are also really useful if you need to shape a blank from a flat piece of metal into a curved cuff, for example, because it allows you to do so without leaving a mark.

Chasing and Texturizing Hammers

Beyond the brass and nylon starter hammers, there are also hammers that will help flatten metals and wire (called chasing hammers) and hammers that will give texture to your blanks (called texturizing hammers). You can experiment with using a chasing hammer on wire when you make the Free-Form Beaded Earrings (see Chapter 5), and you can also hammer the edges of blanks to give them a more polished look when you make the Winter Weather Stud Earrings (see Chapter 5).

Texturizing hammers come in several patterns—lines, dots, swirls, and more—and they're useful when you want to design something using metal blanks that you don't necessarily wish to stamp words or designs on. Because this book focuses specifically on stamping, you won't find texturizing hammers used here. However, if you discover that you really enjoy stamping, it's a natural accessory to create different looks.

Stamps

Stamps, sometimes called punches, are made of hardened metal. They are a few inches long and about the diameter of a pencil, making them easy to hold. They have a design or letter at the bottom where they make contact with your metal blank, and a flat top that you strike with your hammer. The force of a hammer strike on the top of a stamp presses the bottom down and into the metal blank, creating an impression of the design or letter. Stamps come in so many shapes, sizes, fonts, metals, and price points that it can be really overwhelming to choose your first set. This book will take you through the process of choosing stamps—not only choosing the best ones for the projects in the book, but also helping you work out which stamps work best for you! Throughout the projects in this book, you will see the exact set I used to make the project at hand, but feel free to use your favorite font in the size recommended in the materials list to personalize your creation. Stamping is a dynamic art full of options to make each piece your own. There are a few main things to consider when you're choosing your first stamp set.

What Are You Stamping On?

Beginner stampers should typically choose soft metals to start with, because it's easiest to get good impressions on soft metals. Such metals include aluminum, pewter, and silver. Medium-hard metals include nickel, copper, and brass. The difference between these metals depends on the project—nearly any metal is adequate for any project. If you want a heavy look, pewter is a good choice. If you're making something for a friend with allergies to metal or alloys, aluminum is well-tolerated by most people. If you want an aged or vintage look, copper, brass, and silver are great choices. Silver is more expensive than other metals, so be sure to stock up on inexpensive blanks (like aluminum) to get lots of practice in and avoid making a mistake on a pricey blank.

Nearly every stamp set on the market will stamp any of these metals. Standard stamp sets range from $20 to $200, but many designer fonts can be found in the $70 range.

The one metal you cannot stamp with a standard set is stainless steel—some washers, spoons, and other unusual items. To stamp on stainless steel, you'll need a specially hardened stamp set—and it will be marked as premium hardened, for use on all metals including steel.

What Are You Stamping With?

You will have lots of choices when you buy your first set of alphabet stamps. There are different styles—formal or calligraphy script, block, modern, handwritten—and each different style of letters is called a font. Just as you choose a font when typing a document, the font you choose for your stamp set will give your pieces a particular look and feel.

Many new stampers choose a simple, economy-priced block font. This is easy on the budget, but can give your pieces an industrial feel. If you know—or suspect—that you are really going to enjoy stamping, then opt for a font you love! You'll save money in the long run by not buying a set you won't use much. Spending more on a special set gives you features that make stamping easier, like cases that prevent letters from turning or getting mixed up as you work, or even bonus stamps like punctuation marks—perfect for a project liked the Ampersand Ring (see Chapter 2)—and design shapes, like the small dragonfly stamp used in the Dragonfly Charm Earrings (see Chapter 5).

You'll notice throughout this book that there are several fonts featured; these will give you an idea of the variety of fonts available. Each project supply list will note the specific font and size used for that project, but feel free to personalize with your own favorite font or design shape.

In addition to letter sets, there are design stamps in nearly every theme to fit your interest. Basic design stamps like hearts, stars, and flowers are pretty additions to all kinds of pieces, but you'll also find that there are icons and patterns out there for more specific interests as well. Whether you're a dancer, a dog lover, a gardener, or something else entirely, you can find design stamps to suit nearly every passion.

#stampinghacks

Uppercase letters are easiest to work with as a beginner, because each letter is the same height (whereas lowercase letters are different sizes). Sometimes it looks trendy to use all capital letters, but sometimes it just LOOKS LIKE SHOUTING. You'll have to decide what type of look fits your style best.

What Size Stamp Set Do You Need?

To recap what we discussed earlier in this chapter, the science behind metal stamping is this: You are using the force of a hammer to displace the metal under a stamp of a certain size and shape. The larger the stamp or the more details the stamp contains, the more metal you will need to displace. This ultimately means you'll need more force for larger and more complicated stamps. Most letter stamp sets are 3mm–4mm in height, which is an excellent size to start with because it's small enough to fit a phrase on a blank, yet large enough to be legible.

Stamp Straight Tape

One last tool to pick up when you choose your stamps is a roll of ImpressArt's Stamp Straight Tape, which is a heavy, flexible tape that helps you to align your letters. While Stamp Straight Tape is the most effective, if it isn't available in your area, then some masking tape, washi tape, or any type of tape that's easily removable and ¾" wide will work as well. You will need to tape your blanks to your steel block to prevent them from shifting as you stamp, and if you also place some tape where you want to stamp, the tape will help you align your letters. You can mark off letter placement with a fine-tip marker directly on the tape to center your words before you begin, and you can even use the edge of the tape as a baseline for your stamping. You'll learn this technique in detail in Chapter 2.

Other Common Tools

In addition to the must-have tools mentioned in this section, a few more tools used in creating stamped metal jewelry bear mentioning, most of which are used in this book. Not all of these are critical to creating your first stamped pieces, but as you expand your skills and try new techniques, you will often encounter these tools.

Dapping Blocks and Punches

Dapping blocks (also called doming blocks) and punches allow you to curve round blanks, making them concave or convex. The dapping block is a small square wooden or metal block similar to a steel block except that it has several circular hollows covering the surface. Dapping punches are small hammers with spherical tops that match the hollows in the dapping block. Dapping is an easy way to give a basic blank additional depth and shape by placing it in the rounded well of the block and hammering the blank with the matching punches until the blank takes on the curved shape of the well. You can create puffy shapes or cups with domed discs, as you'll see in the Love Bites Puff Pendant in Chapter 3.

Bracelet and Ring Bending Pliers

Bracelet and ring bending pliers allow you to take long, flat blanks and turn them into bracelets and rings, or to shape blanks to be added to bracelets by pressing blanks between curved nylon jaws. Alternately, a bracelet-bending tool helps you to make perfectly curved cuff bracelets. Ring mandrels and anvils can also help in shaping metal blanks by providing a round base, and when used with nylon hammers, allow you to shape small pieces like rings without marring the metal.

Hole Punches

Hole punches are available in two types: hand punches, which are great for higher gauge (thinner) metals, and screw-down punches, which can power through many different gauges of metal. Hand punches are pliers with a special tip that puts a small hole in metal blanks. For thicker blanks, you'll need more muscle than what your hand has, and that's where screw-down punches are necessary. Much like tightening a screw with a screwdriver, the threads inside the punch aid in punching a hole through a metal blank. If you use a blank that isn't pre-drilled or has too small a hole, or if you need to add additional holes, you'll need to invest in at least one type of hole punch. A hand punch is quick and convenient, but screw-down punches offer more versatility and can be used on all projects.

Metal Files

Small metal files are also useful any time you need to punch or drill your own hole, if you cut your metal, or if you use any blank that has a sharp edge. Because jewelry lies against the skin, it's important to file away any sharp edges. A simple, inexpensive set of metal files will work perfectly—you don't need any fancy features, just a file that can blunt potentially sharp edges.

Jewelry-Making Components

Finally, in jewelry-making, you will find that many of the same components are used in each project. Prepare yourself to invest in chain nose pliers, round nose pliers, wire cutters, jump rings in a few different sizes ranging from 4mm to 12mm, clasps, head pins, chain, and a small assortment of beads you love.

MATERIALS

The elements you use in your handmade jewelry are reflections of your own personal style. As you learn techniques, you can easily make changes to the beads, the metal finishes, the fonts and designs used, the color, shape, size, length, weight . . . there are endless options to make a piece truly your own! The same project can look totally different by making simple substitutions, so don't be afraid to experiment with materials that aren't on the supply lists.

Metal Blanks

Each piece in this book has a metal blank as the focal point, so it's important to learn about the different metals available. All metals are not created equal. Metal blanks are the stars of stamped metal jewelry. They are the pieces of metal on which you stamp your word, your name, or your message, and each has different properties. Metal blanks come in a variety of shapes and sizes as well as metals. You can buy bracelet blanks made especially for creating wrist jewelry, round blanks for earrings, blanks with holes already punched in them to create chandelier earrings or attach charms, and many more kinds. When choosing which type of metal blank to use, you will want to consider how easy it is to stamp each type of metal, the best shape for your project, and also the quality and cost of each metal.

Beginner stampers will have the best luck stamping on the softer metals, which include aluminum, pewter, silver, and gold. Some brands of metal blanks are made with special alloys developed for stamped metal jewelry, and these can often be excellent choices. Aluminum blanks are ideal for beginners and for practice, because they are the least expensive—well under a dollar each—and take an impression very well. High-end blanks like gold and silver will naturally be more expensive, and the price will vary based on how large they are.

Copper, brass, and nickel are all harder metals. While they can certainly be stamped, each impression will require more force than when stamping a softer metal. These metals, as well as pewter and various alloys, are between aluminum and silver in price—typically a dollar or two for each blank, depending on the size. These are the metals you'll find used most often in this book because they're economical choices and give you a variety of finishes to match nearly every style. Steel and other hardened metals cannot be stamped with standard stamp sets. There are specially hardened stamps for hard metals out there, but be sure to check that your set is rated for hard metals before trying it, or the hard metal is more likely to flatten your stamp than to take an impression. Steel is typically not used in traditional jewelry, but if you incorporate washers or hardware store metals in your own designs, use caution with hard metals. The hardness of steel can damage standard stamp sets.

The gauge of the metal you work with also makes a difference in your project, but how thick a gauge you will need depends on the hardness of the metal. Gauge matters more for other metalwork; for stamping, any gauge will work. It's only a matter of choosing the gauge best suited to the project or style you are going for. For aluminum, you'll want a lower gauge (a higher thickness) in the 14- to 18-gauge range. Brass and copper, which are harder, hold their shapes at much higher gauges, and working in the 22- to 26-gauge range is perfectly acceptable for many jewelry applications.

#stampinghacks

When giving jewelry gifts, keep in mind that some metals are more allergenic than others. Many times, metals that can be oxidized (like silver, copper, pewter, and brass) cause more reactions for people than aluminum, which does not oxidize.

Darkening Agents

There are several ways to finish stamped metal jewelry pieces to create a special look all your own. One way to personalize is to darken the impressions you stamp into the metal, so that they stand out and are easy to see or read. You have a few different techniques to choose from when darkening your impressions.

Stamp Enamel

In this style of darkening stamped impressions, specially designed stamp enamel is applied to the stamped areas of your blanks and polished clean with a paper towel or shop rag. Stamp enamel is a black liquid that is applied directly to the metal blank after stamping, and then rubbed off with a paper towel or rag. The black enamel will remain in the impressions and the surface of the metal blank will be wiped clean. This technique enables the impressions to really stand out. You will notice that I typically use enamel to finish my stamped blanks in this book, which is strictly a matter of preference. This is an easy method because it requires very little polishing, and still gives you a nearly permanent color. Enamel and paint can be used on any type of metal.

Acrylic Paints

Acrylic paint, when used to darken impressions, works exactly the same as stamp enamel. You apply acrylic paint directly to your stamped metal blank, and polish the excess off the surface with a paper towel or rag. The added bonus of using acrylic paints is that you can darken your letters in any color scheme.

Permanent Markers

Permanent markers also work well for darkening letters and shapes, but typically require more heavy polishing with a polishing cloth. A standard permanent marker can be used to color into the impressions of your piece, and then the surface buffed back to a high shine. The process takes a little more effort to remove all the excess ink from your stamped blank than enamel or paint, but is still a simple alternative. Using permanent marker to darken your impressions only becomes a problem if you're trying to create an aged or vintage look on a piece that's already oxidized, where the amount of polishing needed in using a permanent marker will make your metal look brand new again.

Oxidation

Oxidation is the classic way to finish pieces, and will give you the most authentic vintage look. That natural darkening of reactive metals is called a patina. Using liver of sulfur or another aging patina solution, you can speed up the metal's aging process by exposing it to chemicals. This method often requires lots of polishing with the solution to remove the patina from the entire surface, leaving only the impressions darkened. This is the permanent way to darken your letters and shapes, and it's the method that many purists prefer. However, it's certainly the most time-consuming, and you will often need gloves and a well-ventilated area to oxidize metals in this way.

Finishing your metal blank or your impression by darkening is just one of the detailed and varied ways you can personalize your piece. Next, we'll tackle the basic materials you'll need to create your own beautiful jewelry—in this book and beyond.

Jewelry-Making Materials

These are all of the basic jewelry-making materials you'll need to create the projects in this book. All of these materials can be found at your local craft store or online. Don't be afraid to get creative with these materials! While the specific materials needed to complete the project as shown in this book are noted in each project's materials list, you have a wide assortment of options that will serve the same function but can add your own personal style to a piece. Use the metals that fit your look best, the bead colors and choices that fit your mood, and the chain styles that you love most!

- **Beads:** Beads come in all shapes and sizes, and are a great way to personalize your stamped metal creations. You will add small beads with small stamped metal blanks to create a custom look in the Flirty Charm Bangles project in Chapter 4.
- **Head Pins:** Head pins are short metal wires that end in a pinhead (similar to a pushpin or sewing pin) or small loop. These wires are great for adding beads to your projects—you'll learn how to slide a bead onto a head pin, wrap the wire around itself to secure the bead, and create a loop with which to join it to your project's chain or jump rings.

- **Jump Rings:** Jump rings are small metal loops that form a ring without connecting. The small gap between each end can be twisted open and closed again in order to attach elements to a chain, add beads and charms to a project, and otherwise secure two elements together.
- **Chains:** Chains are not just for pendant necklaces! Throughout the book, you'll learn how to use chains in creative ways to make not only unique necklaces like the Adventurer's Double-Pendant Necklace (see Chapter 3), but intricate bracelets as well.
- **Eyelet Setting Block and Tool:** An eyelet setting block and tool will enable you to punch professional-looking holes through your metal blanks to creatively add charms and amp up the character of your piece by adding a raised element.
- **Rubber Block:** A rubber block is necessary for setting specialty crystal rivets. Similar to a steel block in shape and use, a rubber block is pliable so that the crystals are not harmed when they are set, as in the Shine On Twin-Charm Cuff in Chapter 4.

Now that you know about the tools and supplies you need, it's time to put them to use and learn what you need to do to get started making stamped jewelry! Chapter 2 will show you how to use the essential tools. Stock up on metal blanks (remember, aluminum is a great practice metal) and let's dive in.

CHAPTER 2

Techniques

Hand-stamped jewelry is one of a kind. Because each impression is created individually by hand, it will always be slightly imperfect. Keep this in mind as you begin; even experienced stampers will have slight variations in depth or spacing each time they create a new piece. It's the nature of pieces that are lovingly stamped by hand, rather than machine-pressed or engraved. If your first tries aren't perfect, just remember that in this hobby, these little variations add to the charm and appeal, and make your work special!

I have taught dozens of people how to stamp jewelry, and everyone begins a little differently. Some grab the hammer and can't wait to get started, and others take it slowly, learning as much as possible before that first hammer strike. Keep in mind, you don't need a large steel block to get great results! You can easily move or re-position any blank so that the area you are stamping is supported by the block. Regardless of how you approach a new technique, this chapter will get you stamping clearly and confidently in no time.

The best way to get ahead is to
GET STARTED

stamping letters:

"Quote of the Day"
Cuff Bracelet

materials

WHEN IT COMES to stamping letters, you'll need to learn horizontal alignment (spacing), vertical alignment (keeping letters from being too far up or down), and the force needed for each strike. If you find that you really struggle to develop a confident hammer strike, there are now specialty jigs that will aid you in holding your stamp, so you can focus just on the strike and not split your attention between the hammer and the stamp. This "Quote of the Day" Cuff Bracelet has every challenge that letters can throw at you, and it's best practiced on aluminum, which is one of the most inexpensive metals available. So choose your favorite quote, gather up your tools, and let's get stamping!

- Stamp Straight Tape or washi tape
- 1 (⅜" × 6") 14-gauge aluminum bracelet blank
- Steel block
- Pen or fine-tip marker
- 3mm ImpressArt Newsprint font alphabet stamps, or 3mm alphabet stamps in font of your choice, in upper- and lowercase
- Stamping hammer
- Stamp enamel or acrylic paint
- Paper towel
- Bracelet bending tool

1 **Stamping Set-Up and Lettering Alignment.** To begin, use your Stamp Straight Tape to secure your bracelet blank to your block, with one vertical strip on each end of the blank taping it directly to the block, ensuring that the blank is centered and that both ends are an equal distance from the edges of the block. The top of the wrist is the part of the bracelet that people will be looking at, so that is where your text should be. Whenever possible, limit stamped text to the 2"–3" in the middle of the blank for a bracelet, which means you will need to take a moment to plan your text, allowing for breaks and emphasis.

2 The message for this cuff is "The best way to get ahead is to get started." To add extra emphasis on "get started," you will not only use capital letters, but will also break the text into two lines. Line one will read "The best way to get ahead is to" and line two will read "GET STARTED." You may wish to sketch out your ideas on paper first.

3 **Determine Your Baseline.** Next, determine where you want the bottom of your letters to hit on your blank. This line on which the letters "sit" is the baseline of where you'll be stamping. Adhere a piece of Stamp Straight Tape to the blank at this line. For this project, place the tape parallel to the top and bottom edges of the blank, 4mm from the top edge. The letters in the top line of text will be stamped along the top edge of your tape.

4 **Plan Your Lettering Spacing.** Finally, before you begin, mark off on the tape where you plan to stamp each letter with a pen or fine-tip marker, to double-check that you have space to fit your phrase and that it is centered on the cuff. The exact spacing will vary by font. Some fonts and letters are wider than others, but with a bit of practice, you will learn quickly what spacing you prefer on your pieces. You can also stamp a practice piece to get familiar with the width of your font. Because most letters are nearly 2mm wide in this font, the marks should be placed 2mm apart from each other. This will be slightly narrower than the 3mm width of the stamps themselves.

5 **Letter Stamp Alignment.** To stamp your piece, make sure you have the stamp facing in the correct direction (some stamp brands, like the ones shown in the project photos, are marked with the letters facing toward you, which will help ensure that you never stamp upside down). Place the stamp lightly on your blank, and drag it gently toward the mark on your tape where you plan to stamp it. You will feel the bottom of the letter catch on the edge of the tape, which is how you will know that you have your vertical alignment correct. As long as you also follow the marks on your tape where you wish to stamp each letter, your horizontal alignment will also be correct.

6 **Stamping Uppercase and Lowercase Letters.** Stamping capital letters is relatively easy. They're all the same height, and they're closer to the same width than lowercase letters are. On your first pieces, you may wish to use all capital letters until you're ready to challenge yourself a little more. But when you are ready to include lowercase letters, there are a few things you'll need to know. Letters with descenders ("g," "j," "p," "q," "y") will dip lower than the line of your tape, making it more difficult to place them vertically. As you stamp, it's easiest to simply skip those letters until you've stamped the rest. Then remove the tape, and place it aligned to the top of the smallest letters (like "e," "o," "m," etc.). This time, as you gently place your stamp for letters with descenders, you drag them upward toward the tape instead of downward. Stamp them just as you would any other letter once you've aligned them with the tape.

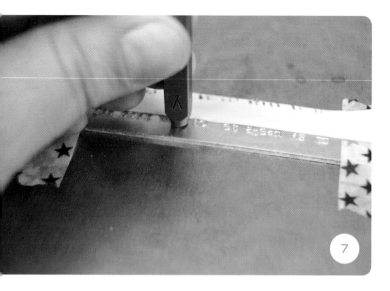

7 **Striking the Stamp.** Hold the stamp as straight upright as possible, and grip it just firmly enough that it won't slip from your hand. Hold it near the bottom, so your hand can rest on the block, helping to steady the stamp that much better. With your hammer, give the top of the stamp one firm tap to create the impression of your letter. Avoid tapping more than once if at all possible. If your hand moves between the taps, you risk getting a double-impression of the letter. You will quickly get a feel for how hard you need to strike the stamp with your hammer by looking at your final piece. If the letters are especially deep, or if the blank warps, you can ease up on your strike. If you have light impressions or if parts of your letters are missing, you need to strike harder. When you begin, try to use the same amount of force that you would when starting to hammer a nail into wood, and make adjustments from there.

8 **Darkening Impressions.** Once you've stamped your piece, it's time to move on to darkening the impressions. Apply the enamel (or paint) by squirting a few lines directly onto the lettering on your piece. Rub in the enamel with a paper towel, making sure it gets all the way into your impressions; wait 10 seconds, then polish it clean. Continue to wipe the piece gently until the surface is cleaned of any enamel, and all that remains are the darkened impressions. If you find that you've accidentally wiped it out of the impressions, you can re-apply it and try again. If this happens, try waiting a few seconds longer the second time before wiping the enamel away.

9 **Bending Metal Blanks.** To finish your cuff, you'll need a bracelet bending tool. Slip one edge of the blank into the groove of the bending tool, and hold the blank tightly with one thumb. Work along the blank, pressing the metal over the curve of the tool until you reach the bend. This will curve one half of the bracelet in the same arc as the bending tool. Then flip the cuff over, and repeat the bend on the other side, giving you a fully curved cuff bracelet. ●

#happystamping

I prefer stamp enamel, but feel free to use another darkening method if you wish—just keep in mind that because aluminum does not tarnish, it cannot be chemically oxidized. You'll have to use enamel, paint, or ink to darken aluminum blanks.

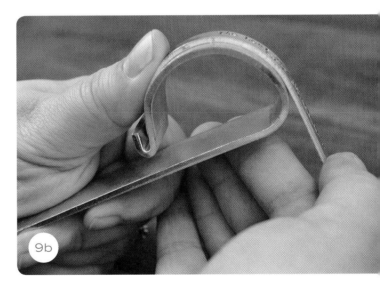

stamping patterns:

Dandelion Wishes
Cuff Bracelet

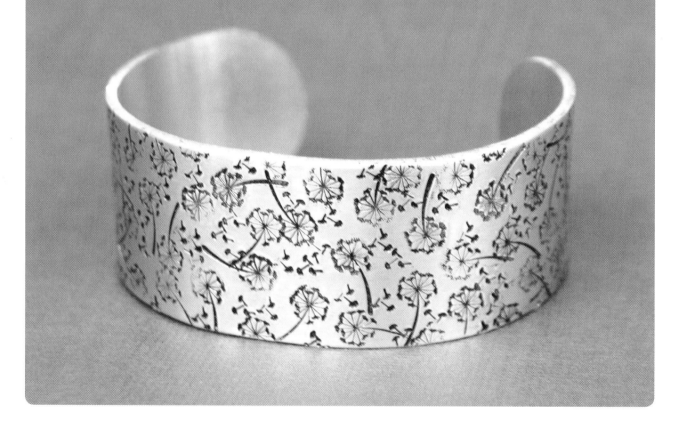

THIS WHIMSICAL BRACELET is simply styled, which makes it a great piece for practicing with larger design stamps. The all-over pattern will camouflage mistakes while letting you get a feel for the amount of force necessary for bigger and more intricate stamps. The larger the stamp and the more detailed it is, the harder you will need to hit it to get a crisp and even impression. And because practice makes perfect, by the time you've covered this cuff in dandelions and fluff, you will have a lot more insight into using big design stamps confidently in your work.

materials

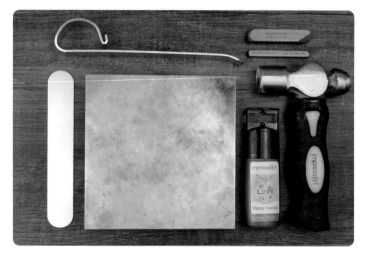

- Stamp Straight Tape or washi tape
- 1 (1" × 6") 14-gauge aluminum bracelet blank
- Steel block
- Beaducation's 11mm and 3mm Dandelion & Fluff Design Stamps set, or any two sizes of coordinating stamps
- Stamping hammer
- Stamp enamel or acrylic paint
- Paper towel
- Bracelet bending tool

1 Tape your bracelet blank to your block so that it stays steady while you stamp. Because you're not stamping any letters, and the goal is an all-over pattern for this project, you may place your tape anywhere. It's only necessary to keep the blank from slipping off the block.

2 **Stamping with Non-Letter Shapes.** Take your large stamp and hold it steady and upright against the bracelet blank. With large stamps like this, you should be able to feel that it's making even contact with your blank. Use your hammer to strike the top of the stamp with full force, which is a harder strike than you would use for letters. Then move the stamp aside and check your result. If you have a crisp impression, then you will repeat the same strike each time you use this stamp. If you find that the impression is too light, you'll need to strike a little harder. If part of the impression is lighter or missing altogether, then make an effort to hold the stamp straighter before striking.

3 **Creating a Stamped Pattern.** Fill in the entire cuff blank with your large stamp. Stamp over the edges in some places, and don't forget to rotate and turn your stamp as you go so that you have flowers from every direction. This will give you the random, all-over look.

4 Next, go back over the cuff with the small stamp, filling in any small gaps in your pattern. Again, be sure to rotate the stamp as you go to make it look more natural.

5 Apply the enamel or paint, as we learned in the "Quote of the Day" Cuff Bracelet, by squirting a few lines directly onto your piece. Rub in the enamel with a paper towel, making sure it gets all the way into your impressions; wait 10 seconds, then polish it clean. Continue to wipe the piece gently until the surface is cleaned, and all that remains are the darkened impressions. If you find that you've accidentally wiped it out of the impressions, you can re-apply it and try again. If this happens, try waiting a few seconds longer the second time before wiping the enamel away.

6 **Complete Your Project.** To finish your cuff, slip one edge of the blank into the groove of the bending tool, and hold the blank tightly with one thumb. Work along the blank, pressing the metal over the curve of the tool until you reach the bend. This will curve one half of the bracelet in the same arc as the bending tool. Then flip the cuff over, and repeat the bend on the other side, giving you a fully curved cuff bracelet. The great textured look makes this cuff an everyday piece for any wardrobe. ●

#stampinghacks

If you find that you end up with a partial stamp, and one side is missing or very light, then your stamp wasn't 100% straight. If you find that it skipped or left a double impression, that's caused by hesitation or an unsteady hand. But you can cover mistakes easily with this flexible design.

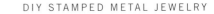

stamping texture:

Smart Is Sexy Owl Necklace

WITTY CONVERSATION IS the best element of a great date, because smart is sexy. Don't you agree? Your owl friend is here to tell the world that you won't settle for a pretty smile, if the brain behind it can't keep up with you! In this design, you'll begin to incorporate different textures and layers into your work to make a piece with depth that isn't difficult.

materials

- 1 (1¼") round aluminum blank
- Steel block
- Stamp Straight Tape
- Stamping hammer
- 1 (6mm) circle design stamp
- 1 (36mm) owl brass blank, treated with patina
- Pen or fine-tip marker
- 3mm ImpressArt Newsprint font alphabet stamps, or 3mm alphabet stamps in font of your choice, in uppercase

- Nylon hammer
- Buffing pad or buffing block
- 1–2 beads, 3mm–6mm in size
- 1 (2") brass jewelry head pin
- Round nose pliers
- Wire cutters
- Chain nose pliers
- 2 (7mm) brass jump rings
- 1 (24", 2mm) brass necklace chain

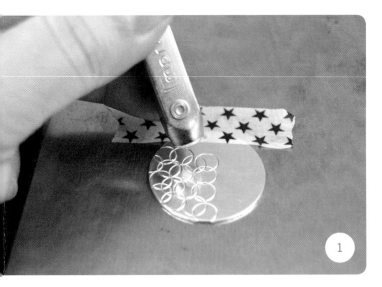

1 **Stamping Texture.** Prepare your round "background" blank by taping it to your steel block with Stamp Straight Tape in one vertical line on the left side of the blank. Move the tape as needed to stamp the entire blank. Using your stamping hammer, stamp the blank repeatedly with a 6mm circle design stamp, overlapping the circles as you go for a random-looking texture, covering the entire blank with circles. These overlapping circles hint at a nest shape. It may not look like much on its own, but the contrasting metal and the texture will help your blank stand out when you've finished your piece.

2 Next, stamp your owl blank. Mark off your message using Stamp Straight Tape, lining up a piece of tape where the bottom of your letters will be placed. Map out your "SMART IS SEXY" message in the center of your owl blank, both vertically and horizontally, on three lines (one for each word). Begin with the top line, "SMART." Remove the tape after stamping your first word, and move it down the blank 4–5mm. Stamp your second line, "IS," and move the tape again for the final line, "SEXY." After adding the message, you can experiment with adding detail to your owl with any 3mm stamps, if you like! I used lowercase "o's" to give the owl eyes; you can also stamp an uppercase "V" to create a nice beak, and a few well-placed "u's" to add feathers to the wings.

3 **Correcting Accidentally Curved Thin Metal Blanks.**
Because brass is a medium-hard metal, the
blanks are often strong and thin. But thin blanks
can curve a bit as you stamp them; this is
typical. If it should happen to you, turn the blank
over and hammer the back side flat with a nylon
hammer without taping the blank to the block.
This won't mar your blank, but it will flatten it
back out nicely.

4 Next, buff the blank with the buffing pad or
buffing block—both of which are essentially
extra fine–grit sanding pads—until you've got
the amount of shine you wish to show. This brass
blank with patina already added is a bit different
than polished blanks. In this case, instead of
adding a darkening agent, we'll be buffing away
some of the patina to reveal the impressions,
leaving an organic, distressed look that pairs
well with nature-themed pieces like this one.
Go lightly and check the blank often as you buff;
you can't put it back on once you've removed it if
you get the blank too shiny.

5 **Adding a Charm.** The next step is to create a beaded charm to add to your necklace. To make a beaded charm, add 1–2 small beads onto a 2" jewelry head pin. Grip the head pin with your round nose pliers just above the top bead. Wrap the wire end of the head pin around one side of your pliers, forming a loop.

6 Next, take the wire end of the head pin with your fingers or a set of pliers, and wrap it around the head pin under the loop you created. Wrap it in neat coils around the wire until the space between the loop and the top of the bead has been filled. There's no minimum number of wraps for your charm to be secure; as long as it wraps around just once, it will be strong enough to hold up to regular wear. Additional wraps are just to fill the gap instead of allowing the bead to slide around.

7 If there's any excess wire when you're done wrapping, trim it off with wire cutters. Note: take caution when cutting small pieces of wire; they don't always drop to the table and may fly into the air. Ensure you collect and dispose of all remnant pieces. If any bit of wire is sticking out that may catch on clothing after you've trimmed it, press it down with your chain nose pliers so that it wraps snugly around the base of the head pin.

8 Finally, assemble your elements to finish your necklace. Twist open a 7mm jump ring with your chain nose pliers by using two sets of pliers to grab on either side of the seam in the ring. Twist the pliers and ends of the jump ring away from each other in a north-south motion. Slide the beaded charm onto the jump ring, then close the ring by twisting the ends back toward each other so the ends of the ring are flush. Then open a second medium-sized jump ring in the same way, and layer the textured round blank, owl charm, and beaded charm onto this ring; close the ring as you did the previous one. String the closed ring onto a 24" brass necklace chain, and your wise owl necklace is ready for wear! ●

#happystamping

Experiment with variations on textured pieces by adding light patinas or alcohol inks to the surface, and blotting or buffing them back to a near-shine.

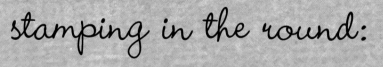

stamping in the round:

Hot Stuff Coffee Locket

materials

IF YOU CAN'T function without your coffee (ahem, guilty), then you're going to love this sassy locket! You'll never be without coffee when you wear this surprisingly simple necklace. The best part about these charm lockets is that you can change the contents anytime you like, so one locket can be worn with any message just by stamping a new disc. In this piece, I'm sharing my secret for stamping in the round, which is a technique you can use when you stamp any disc.

- ⅝" circle paper punch
- 1 small (⅝" diameter) circle of craft vinyl
- 1 (⅞") round aluminum blank
- Steel block
- Stamp Straight Tape
- 3mm ImpressArt Bridgette font alphabet stamps, or 3mm alphabet stamps in font of your choice, in lowercase

- Stamping hammer
- Stamp enamel
- Paper towel
- 3–5 coffee beans
- 1 (30mm) glass floating charm locket
- Small knife or file (optional)
- 1 (30", 2mm) gold chain
- 1 (4mm) gold jump ring
- Chain nose pliers

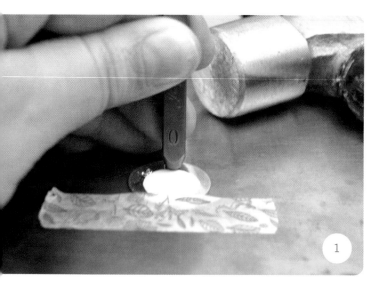

1 **Stamping in the Round.** Use your paper punch to cut a ⅝" circle out of your craft vinyl. Place the vinyl onto the center of your round blank to guide the placement of your letters, just as Stamp Straight Tape does when stamping letters in a straight line. Secure your round blank to the steel block with tape to hold it still while you stamp your message, "hey hot stuff," in the next step.

2 Align each stamp along the edge of the vinyl circle, just as you would when stamping a straight line using Stamp Straight Tape. You may find it helpful to mark the placement of each letter before beginning on the vinyl circle with a pen, though because this project uses a round disc, you will not need to worry about centering the phrase. There is no specific top or bottom to the circle until the message has been stamped.

3 Just as in the "Quote of the Day" Cuff Bracelet, this message has a letter that descends below your vinyl circle baseline. As you stamp, skip over the letter "y" in the word "hey." When you have stamped all the other letters, remove the vinyl from your blank. Place a small piece of tape at the top of where you will stamp the letter "y," using the top of the neighboring letter "e" to gauge the height. Drag the "y" stamp upward toward the tape, and when you feel the edge, stamp your final letter to finish your round disc.

#stampinghacks

When stamping on the round, you can't really use Stamp Straight Tape to aid your letter placement, but you can apply the same technique by using a small scrap of vinyl cut in a circle! 3mm letters need a margin of ⅛" all the way around; cut or punch a piece of vinyl that is ¼" smaller than the blank you're stamping. In this case—a ⅝" circle is perfect for the ⅞" aluminum disc, because I'm using a 3mm font.

4   Apply the enamel by squirting a few lines directly onto your piece. Rub in the enamel with a paper towel, making sure it gets all the way into your impressions; wait 10 seconds, then polish it clean. Continue to wipe the piece gently until the surface is cleaned of any enamel, and all that remains are the darkened impressions. If you find that you've accidentally wiped it out of the impressions, you can re-apply it and try again. If this happens, try waiting a few seconds longer the second time before wiping the enamel away.

5   Next, add coffee beans to the locket to complete the piece! Coffee beans can vary in size, so if you find that the locket won't quite close, you can use a small knife or file on the back side of the bean to shave just enough off to fit the locket.

6   Connect the two ends of the 30" chain together with a jump ring. Twist open a 4mm jump ring with your chain nose pliers by using two sets of pliers to grab on either side of the seam in the ring. Twist the pliers and ends of the jump ring away from each other in a north-south motion. Slide each side of the chain onto the jump ring, then close the ring by twisting the ends back toward each other so the ends of the ring are flush. Slip the long chain over your head for wear! ●

using rivets

and eyelets:

Natural Beauty Necklace

materials

ONCE YOU'VE WORKED your way through some of the easier designs in this book, there are some additional elements that you can add to stamped metal, like rivets and eyelets, which will give your piece a great finished look. Rivets and eyelets are small punches that add character to your piece—a rivet looks almost like a thick thumbtack while an eyelet creates a bordered hole through your metal blank. When you feel ready to move beyond stamping and take your designs to the next level, the mixed metals in this "natural beauty" necklace make it look anything but handmade!

- 1 (1½") oval pewter blank with 2 (³⁄₃₂") holes
- Steel block
- Stamp Straight Tape or washi tape
- Pen or fine-tip marker
- 3mm ImpressArt Bridgette font alphabet stamps, or 3mm lowercase alphabet stamps in font of your choice
- Stamping hammer
- 3mm heart design stamp
- Stamp enamel
- Paper towel
- Eyelet setting block and tool

- Eyelets: 1 (3.7mm) copper and 1 (5.3mm) silver
- 1 copper finish rivetable floral element with 2mm center hole
- 1 round copper bead
- 1 (2") silver finish jewelry eye pin
- Round nose pliers
- Wire cutters
- 2 (4mm) silver jump rings
- Chain nose pliers
- 1 silver leaf bead
- 1 (15mm) silver jump ring
- 1 (24", 2mm) silver finish necklace chain

1 Adhere your pewter blank to your steel block with the oval oriented with the holes at the top and bottom of the blank with Stamp Straight Tape. Place the tape where the bottom of each of the 7 letters will be stamped on the first line, just above the center of your blank. Use your pen or fine-tip marker to mark off the placement of your letters. Stamp the word "natural," then remove the tape. Move the Stamp Straight Tape down to the second line, marking 6 letters on the tape. Stamp the word "beauty" and remove the tape again. Finally, move your tape down to the third line, and at the center point, stamp a single 3mm heart.

2 Apply the enamel by squirting a few lines directly onto your piece. Rub in the enamel with a paper towel, making sure it gets all the way into your impressions; wait 10 seconds, then polish it clean. Continue to wipe the piece gently until the surface is cleaned of any enamel, and all that remains are the darkened impressions. If you find that you've accidentally wiped it out of the impressions, you can re-apply it and try again. If this happens, try waiting a few seconds longer the second time before wiping the enamel away.

3   **Setting Eyelets.** Don't let the idea of setting eyelets intimidate you. The holes that come on your blank must be at least ³⁄₃₂"—if they're not, you may need to use a hole punch to expand them slightly. Place the rounded side of the eyelet on the groove in the eyelet setting block, and use your steel block as a sturdy base. Set the lower hole of the blank over the small 3.7mm copper eyelet, fitting it onto the eyelet so that the small end protrudes through the blank.

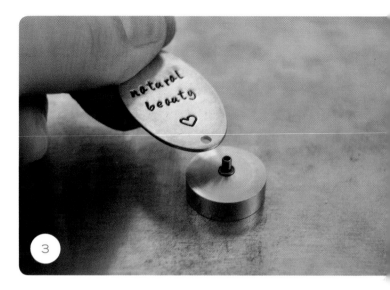

4   Position the eyelet setting tool inside the hole of the eyelet and tap the top of it several times with your hammer. The tool has a rounded groove so that you can smoothly flare the eyelet over the edge of the hole. Set the larger 5.3mm eyelet at the top of the blank in the same way, stacking the rivetable flower on top of the blank before setting the eyelet. You will connect these two pieces permanently together when you set this larger eyelet.

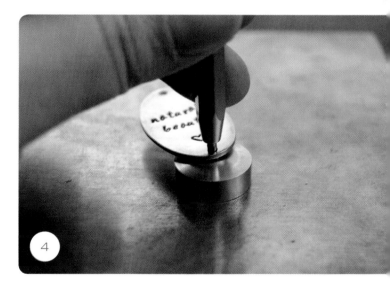

5 The next step is to create a beaded connector or charm to add to your necklace. To do this, add a small round copper bead to a 2" eye pin. Grip the pin with your round nose pliers just above the bead, and wrap the top of the pin around one side of your pliers, forming a loop. Use your wire cutters to cut away the excess wire under the loop on this side of the pin, so that the loop closes snugly at the top of the bead.

6 Twist open a 4mm jump ring with your chain nose pliers by using two sets of pliers to grab on either side of the seam in the ring. Twist the pliers and ends of the jump ring away from each other in a north-south motion. Slide the leaf bead onto the jump ring, then close the ring by twisting the ends back toward each other so the ends of the ring are flush, creating the leaf charm.

7 Connect the leaf bead charm to one side of the beaded connector you created in the previous step with a 4mm jump ring. Then, add the opposite side of the beaded connector to the bottom of the pendant with another 4mm jump ring. Connect the large 15mm jump ring at the top of the pendant, and string it onto the chain. ●

#happystamping

Vertical pendants often look best on chains 24" or longer, but making these pieces yourself means that you can adjust them to suit your own tastes. String the pendant, and wow your friends with this impressive two-finish design.

mixing stamping and leather:
Untamed Leather Bracelet

DIY STAMPED METAL JEWELRY

I LOVE THE organic look of leather cords—it always reminds me of nature and wildlife. The sentiment "untamed" comes to mind, so I created a rustic design to venture down the road of leather jewelry, which pairs nicely with stamped metal. This simple design technique can be personalized to fit any size wrist and any kind of sentiment, making it a versatile design for gifts (and of course, gifts to yourself)!

materials

- 1 (1⅜") pewter oval blank with 2 (4mm) holes
- Steel block
- Stamp Straight Tape or washi tape
- Pen or fine-tip marker
- 3mm ImpressArt Newsprint font alphabet stamps, or 3mm alphabet stamps in font of your choice, in upper- and lowercase
- Stamping hammer
- Stamp enamel
- Paper towel
- Bracelet bending pliers
- 16" (2mm) leather cord, cut into 2 (8") pieces
- 1 silver finish glue-on end clasp with 3–4mm opening
- Heavy-duty adhesive (like E6000)

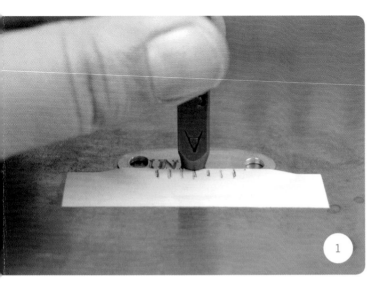

1 Adhere your pewter blank to your steel block with Stamp Straight Tape, placing it where the bottom of the 7 letters will be stamped for the word "UNTAMED." Use your pen or fine-tip marker to mark off the placement of each letter, and then stamp them.

2 Apply the enamel by squirting a few lines directly onto your piece. Rub in the enamel with a paper towel, making sure it gets all the way into your impressions; wait 10 seconds, then polish it clean. Continue to wipe the piece gently until the surface is cleaned of any enamel, and all that remains are the darkened impressions. If you find that you've accidentally wiped it out of the impressions, you can re-apply it and try again. If this happens, try waiting a few seconds longer the second time before wiping the enamel away.

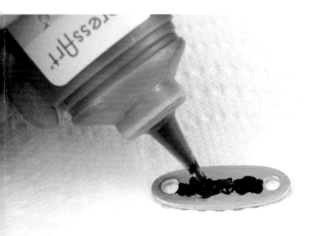

3 Curve the blank to fit your wrist by pressing it with bracelet bending pliers. With the letters facing the concave side of the pliers, squeeze it firmly between the two nylon pads. This will curve the stamped blank gently in a smooth and uniform way.

2

4   **Attaching Leather Cord.** Double one of your 8" pieces of leather cord, and push the fold through one side of your stamped oval blank. Then feed the tails through this fold, creating a loop around the outside of the blank called a lark's head knot. Pull it tight, and repeat the knot on the opposite side.

5   The next step may vary based on how long you need your bracelet to be. Measure the length of the clasp past where the leather will be glued in. For example, the clasp shown is 3" long with ½" wells for the leather to glue into. Since the clasp adds length to my final piece, I'll need to account for how deeply the leather tucks into the clasp. Cut your leather pieces each to a length of 6", and glue each side into the well of the clasp.

6   Allow the glue to dry completely so it is secure, a few hours to overnight, and your bracelet is ready for wear! ●

#stampinghacks

If I am making a finished bracelet that is 7½" long, and the wells in the clasp are ¾" deep, I will need to add ¾" of length to each end of leather to compensate. Then I would subtract the length of the clasp, which is 3" in this case. I would know that I need to cut my leather bracelet to a length of 6", with the stamped oval blank centered in the middle.

*darkening stamped blanks
with enamel, ink,
or acrylic paints:*

Ampersand Ring

ARE YOU THE kind of girl who's always looking for more? The ampersand—the "and" symbol—is the ultimate clue that there's more to come, or it highlights a great pairing. Surf & Turf. Milk & Cookies. You & Me. This simple ring is a great way to practice your design stamping and darkening stamped blanks, plus the dual metals make for a combination to match everything.

materials

- 1 (½") copper circle blank
- Steel block
- 6mm ImpressArt Ampersand Design Stamp
- Stamping hammer
- Stamp Straight Tape (optional)
- Stamp enamel or acrylic paint
- Paper towel
- Adjustable silver finish bezel ring with ½" well
- Heavy-duty adhesive (like E6000)

1 Place your copper blank onto your steel block. Align your ampersand stamp by sight on the center of your blank. Stamp the ampersand on your blank with your stamping hammer. When working with large or detailed design stamps, remember that you have to strike harder, and be sure that your stamp is perfectly flat on the surface of your blank. You may wish to tape your blank to your block to ensure that it doesn't shift when you're first practicing.

2 **Darkening Large Impressions.** Apply the enamel or paint by squirting a few lines directly onto your piece. Rub in the enamel with a paper towel, making sure it gets all the way into your impressions; wait 10 seconds, then polish it clean. Continue to wipe the piece gently until the surface is cleaned of any enamel, and all that remains are the darkened impressions. If you find that you've accidentally wiped it out of the impressions, you can re-apply it and try again. If this happens, try waiting a few seconds longer the second time before wiping the enamel away.

3 Assemble the ring by gluing the disc into the bezel with a heavy-duty adhesive like E6000. A little goes a long way; you won't need more than a dab! Allow it to dry fully, according to package directions, which can be anywhere from a few hours to overnight. Let the world know you're ready for more with this easy accessory! ●

using patinas:

Be You Bracelet

I **MENTIONED IN** the Untamed Leather Bracelet tutorial how much I like to pair leather with stamped metal, and this bracelet is one of the perfect reasons why. You can take your stamped creations to the next level with colored patinas, opening up a world beyond silver, brass, and copper. There are several techniques working together in this design, but they all build on the previous projects in this chapter. If you've been working on some of the other pieces, you'll find that much of this design is familiar already.

materials

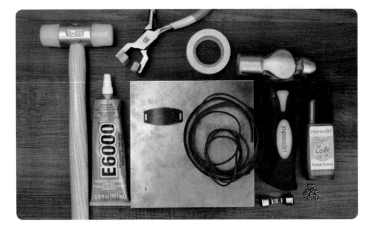

- 1 (45mm × 20mm) brass bracelet blank with 2 (4mm × 2mm) holes, treated with patina

- Nylon hammer

- Steel block

- Stamp Straight Tape

- Pen or fine-tip marker

- 3mm ImpressArt Newsprint font alphabet stamps, or 3mm alphabet stamps in font of your choice, in upper- and lowercase

- Stamping hammer

- Buffing pad or buffing block

- Stamp enamel

- Paper towel

- Patinas for metal—quartz and amethyst

- Disposable cup

- Sponge paintbrush

- Bracelet bending pliers

- 13½" (2mm) round leather cord, cut into 2 (8") pieces

- 10 (4mm) gold metal beads with 2mm hole

- 13½" (10mm) flat leather cord, cut into 2 (6¾") pieces

- Heavy-duty adhesive (like E6000)

- 1 gold glue-on end clasp with 10mm opening

1 Flatten out the brass bracelet blank with a nylon hammer before stamping by turning the blank onto the steel block with the ends curved up and stamp them down toward the block.

2 This bracelet reads: "be bold. be confident. be gentle. be kind. be wise. be unique. be the best. BE YOU." This large rectangle blank can hold 4 lines of text, and this message fills it!

Before beginning, lay the blank on your steel block, and flatten it using your nylon hammer. Once flat, adhere your brass blank to the steel block with Stamp Straight Tape, placing it where the bottom of the top row of letters will be stamped. Use your pen or fine-tip marker to mark off the placement of the words, "be bold. be confident." and stamp these letters.

Move the Stamp Straight Tape to the next line, marking off the message, "be gentle. be kind." As you stamp this second line, skip over the descending letter "g" and stamp the other letters. When you have finished this line, remove the tape, and replace it at the top of where you will stamp the "g," using the neighboring "e" as a guide for where the top of the letter should be placed. Using the bottom of the Stamp Straight Tape to align the letter, stamp the "g," and move on to the third line of text.

Mark off the letters for the message, "be wise. be unique." Just as with the "g" in the second line, skip over the "q" in "unique," then go back and stamp it when you're finished with the line, using the neighboring "u" to aid in placing the tape.

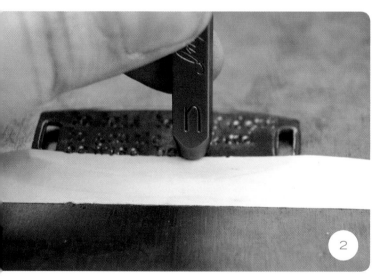

Finally, move the tape to the bottom of the blank and mark off the spacing for "be the best. BE YOU." Stamp the first phrase in lowercase letters, and for the final and most important message, "BE YOU," switch to capital letters and stamp the last two words.

3 When you've filled your blank, buff the blank lightly with the buffing pad or buffing block to remove some of the natural patina and allow some of the brass beneath to shine through.

4 Apply the enamel by squirting a few lines directly onto your piece. Rub in the enamel with a paper towel, making sure it gets all the way into your impressions; wait 10 seconds, then polish it clean. Continue to wipe the piece gently until the surface is cleaned of any enamel, and all that remains are the darkened impressions. If you find that you've accidentally wiped it out of the impressions, you can re-apply it and try again. If this happens, try waiting a few seconds longer the second time before wiping the enamel away.

5 **Applying Artificial Patinas.** Mix the two patina colors together in a disposable cup. Then lightly brush a dime-sized amount of the mixed-color patina to your piece with the sponge brush. Brush the patina lightly across the top of your blank and avoid getting any into your letter impressions, and allow to dry.

6 Curve the blank back into shape by pressing it with bracelet bending pliers, with the letters facing outward.

7 Next, double one of your 8" pieces of 2mm leather cord, and push the fold through one side of your stamped blank. Then feed the tails through this fold, creating a loop on the outside of your blank, called a lark's head knot. Pull it tight, and repeat the knot on the opposite side with the other 8" cord.

8 Add the small metal beads with large holes to the 2mm leather strands.

9   Next, create the bracelet's strap by layering one length of 10mm leather on top of the other, and the 2mm cords on top of that. Gather these ends, and glue them into one side of the end clasp.

10   Finally, glue the other end of the clasp to your bracelet. To highlight the layers of leather, cross one end of the leather over the other before gluing it in place. This will cause it to fan out in the front, instead of being stacked neatly. Allow the glue to dry fully, according to package directions, and your bracelet is ready for anything . . . are you? ●

#stampinghacks

If you make a mistake or don't like your work, it's no problem! If the patina is still wet, you should be able to wipe it off. If it has begun to dry, you may need to buff it off. You can also layer on more to correct mistakes. Just paint your piece until you're happy with it, and allow it to dry for at least 10 minutes before continuing.

CHAPTER 3

Necklaces

The first thing that many people envision when they think about stamped metal jewelry is the classic charm necklace. While necklaces are a staple accessory for nearly every wardrobe, that doesn't mean that stamped jewelry is strictly one style! In this chapter, you can explore designs from classic to trendy, and sweet to sassy. Social media mavens will love the Hashtag Fabulous Bar Necklace, the curious can experiment with the Adventurer's Double-Pendant Necklace, and the dreamers will fall in love with the Unicorn Magic Necklace.

Explore working with different metals and sizes, and use a variety of techniques until you find your favorite style and create a signature piece of your own. In this chapter, you will find projects that range from beginner to intermediate skill levels to keep you inspired no matter where you're at with your stamping.

Hashtag Fabulous Bar Necklace

DIY STAMPED METAL JEWELRY

YOU KNOW WHAT'S trending now? Bar necklaces! They're a simple accessory that lets you express yourself, and now that you're stamping, you can make one for every mood. Stock up on metal blanks—heavier pewter is an excellent choice—and start making something #fabulous.

materials

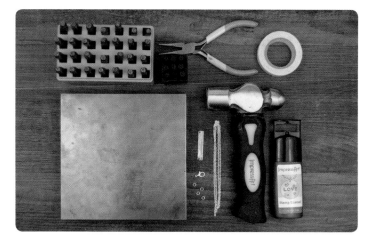

- 1 (½") pewter bar blank
- Steel block
- Stamp Straight Tape or washi tape
- Pen or fine-tip marker
- 3mm ImpressArt Newsprint font alphabet stamps, or 3mm alphabet stamps in font of your choice, in lowercase
- 3mm punctuation stamps
- Stamping hammer
- Stamp enamel or acrylic paint
- Paper towel
- 4 (4mm) silver jump rings
- Chain nose pliers
- 1 (16", 2mm) silver finish chain, cut into 2 (8") lengths
- 1 (12mm) silver lobster clasp

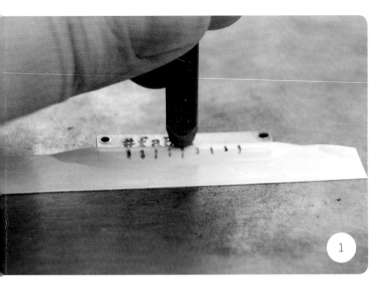

1 Adhere your pewter blank to your steel block with Stamp Straight Tape, placing it where the bottom of the letters will be stamped. Use your pen or fine-tip marker to mark off the placement of your letters, then stamp "#fabulous" on the bar blank.

2 Apply the enamel (or paint) by squirting a few lines directly onto your piece. Rub in the enamel with a paper towel, making sure it gets all the way into your impressions; wait 10 seconds, then polish it clean. Continue to wipe the piece gently until the surface is cleaned of any enamel, and all that remains are the darkened impressions. If you find that you've accidentally wiped it out of the impressions, you can re-apply it and try again. If this happens, try waiting a few seconds longer the second time before wiping the enamel away.

3 Finish your necklace by attaching 8" of chain to each side of the bar with small jump rings. Twist open a 4mm jump ring with your chain nose pliers by using two sets of pliers to grab on either side of the seam in the ring. Twist the pliers and ends of the jump ring away from each other in a north-south motion. Slide the stamped metal blank and the end of one 8" chain onto the jump ring, then close the ring by twisting the ends back toward each other so the ends of the ring are flush. Repeat the jump ring attachment on the other side of the metal blank with another length of chain. On the other end of each 8" chain, repeat the jump ring process twice more to attach each piece of the lobster clasp to each end of the necklace. Then let everyone know how #fabulous you are when you wear this great little piece! ●

Sugar and Spice Charm Necklace

materials

SO, BE HONEST, are you more sugar or spice? This necklace has every girl covered with two stamped pendants. This necklace is a great beginner project because you'll be using all capital letters and stamping straight across the center of these sassy charms for a fun, everyday accessory.

- 2 (¾") round brass blanks, treated with patina
- Steel block
- Stamp Straight Tape
- Pen or fine-tip marker
- 3mm ImpressArt Basic Metal Stamp Set, in uppercase, or 3mm alphabet stamps in font of your choice, in uppercase
- Stamping hammer
- Buffing pad or buffing block
- 1 (4mm) faceted crystal bead
- 1 (2mm) faceted crystal bead
- 1 (2") brass jewelry head pin
- Round nose pliers
- Wire cutters
- Chain nose pliers
- 3 (7mm) brass finish jump rings
- 1 (24", 2mm) brass necklace chain with clasp

1 Adhere the first brass blank to your steel block with Stamp Straight Tape, placing it where the bottom of the letters for "SUGAR" will be stamped, directly in the center of your blank. Use your pen or fine-tip marker to mark off the placement of your letters. Stamp the first blank with "SUGAR" and repeat the same process for the second blank, stamping "SPICE."

2 To create the distressed effect shown, buff the blanks with the buffing pad or buffing block until you've got the amount of shine you wish to show. Go lightly and check the blank often as you buff; you can't put it back on once you've removed it if you get the blank too shiny.

3 Now you are ready to create a beaded charm to add to your necklace. To make a beaded charm, add the two crystal beads onto a 2" jewelry head pin. Grip the head pin above the beads with your round nose pliers, and wrap the wire end of the head pin around one side of your pliers, forming a loop.

#stampinghacks

Brass blanks with patina already on them are slightly different than using polished blanks. In this case, instead of adding a darkening agent, we'll be buffing away some of the patina to reveal the impressions. It makes for a distressed effect, instead of being bright and shiny. This project could also be made with more traditional blanks as well; it all depends on your tastes!

4   Next, take the wire end of the head pin with your fingers or a set of pliers, and wrap it around the head pin under the loop you created. Wrap it in neat coils around the wire until the space between the loop and the top of the bead has been filled. There's no minimum number of wraps for your charm to be secure; as long as it wraps around just once, it will be strong enough to hold up to regular wear. Additional wraps are just to fill the gap instead of allowing the bead to slide around.

5   If there's any excess wire when you're done wrapping it, trim it off with wire cutters. Note: take caution when cutting small pieces of wire; they don't always drop to the table and may fly into the air. Ensure you collect and dispose of all remnant pieces. If any bit of wire is sticking out that may catch on clothing after you've trimmed it, press it down with your chain nose pliers so that it wraps snugly around the base of the head pin.

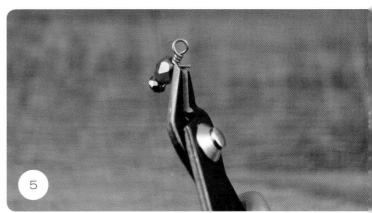

6   Finally, add your stamped blanks and beaded charm onto the chain. To attach the charms, twist open each 7mm jump ring with your chain nose pliers by using two sets of pliers to grab on either side of the seam in the ring. Twist the pliers and ends of the jump rings away from each other in a north-south motion. Slide each of the stamped metal blanks and beaded charm onto its own jump ring, then close each ring by twisting the ends back toward each other so the ends of the ring are flush. Finally, you can just string these charms onto your chain to finish your necklace. ●

Unicorn Magic Necklace

ONE OF THE classic stamped jewelry canvases is the round washer. It's whimsical, and it allows for a wide variety of charms and additions. You can get as wild as you like with this design, adding, for example, a magical bucking unicorn, and a sassy sentiment to match! You'll begin with uppercase stamps here for this great beginner necklace.

materials

- 1 (1½") aluminum washer
- Steel block
- Stamp Straight Tape or washi tape
- 3mm ImpressArt Juniper font alphabet stamps, or 3mm alphabet stamps in font of your choice, in uppercase
- Stamping hammer
- 3mm whimsical star design stamp included in ImpressArt Juniper font alphabet stamps uppercase set
- Stamp enamel
- Paper towel
- 1 (12mm) silver finish jump ring
- Chain nose pliers
- 1 (¾") unicorn charm
- 1 (18", 2mm) silver finish necklace chain with clasp

1 Begin by taping your washer to your steel block at any point with your Stamp Straight Tape, simply to secure it while you're stamping.

2 Center your stamp vertically along the washer, making sure it does not hang over the top or bottom edge, and stamp the message "I BELIEVE IN UNICORN MAGIC" on the bottom point of the round washer. As you move along the washer, rotate your steel block, so that you're always stamping at the very bottom point. By rotating your block, you're most likely to stamp every letter straight. If you try to turn the stamp as you go around, you're much more likely to get some crooked letters. If you find that your message doesn't fill the washer completely, you can fill the empty space on the washer with a few whimsical stars.

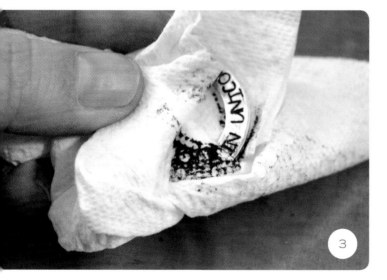

3 Apply the enamel by squirting a few lines directly onto your piece. Rub in the enamel with a paper towel, making sure it gets all the way into your impressions; wait 10 seconds, then polish it clean. Continue to wipe the piece gently until the surface is cleaned of any enamel, and all that remains are the darkened impressions. If you find that you've accidentally wiped it out of the impressions, you can re-apply it and try again. If this happens, try waiting a few seconds longer the second time before wiping the enamel away.

4 Finally, twist open the 12mm jump ring with your chain nose pliers by using two sets of pliers to grab on either side of the seam in the ring. Twist the pliers and ends of the jump ring away from each other in a north-south motion. Slide the stamped washer and the charm onto the ring, then close the ring by twisting the ends back toward each other so the ends of the ring are flush. The charm will hang lower into the center of the washer, and the washer will rest right on top, so both will be easily visible when worn. String the ring onto an 18" silver necklace chain with clasp for a jewelry piece that's a great conversation starter! ●

#stampinghacks

Don't be nervous about not having your tape as your safety net! Slim blanks and washers can often be easier to stamp than larger areas, as long as you take your time when placing each stamp. The uppercase font will also give you a nice uniform size for the whole message.

Adventurer's Double-Pendant Necklace

CONFESSION: I AM smitten with layered necklaces. I rarely wear just one necklace on its own. This piece was designed for you adventurers out there who love the look of two necklaces—with none of the eventual tangles. This piece sports one stamped vertical bar paired with a coordinated bead charm, but don't forget that you really have free rein when adapting this design to suit your personality and style! Choose a long tube-shaped bead or stack several small beads together when creating your bead charm, because vertical shapes catch the eye, even with small or simple elements.

materials

- 1 (1½" × ⅜") 4-sided pewter rectangle bar charm
- Stamp Straight Tape or washi tape
- Steel block
- 3mm ImpressArt Bridgette font alphabet stamps, or 3mm alphabet stamps in font of your choice, in lowercase
- Stamping hammer
- 3mm heart design stamp, or a 3mm design stamp of your choice
- Stamp enamel
- Paper towel
- 1 (2mm) crystal bead

- 1 (15mm) tube-shaped bead
- 2" silver finish jewelry head pin
- Round nose pliers
- Wire cutters
- Chain nose pliers
- 1 (12mm) silver finish jump ring
- 5 (7mm) silver finish jump rings
- Ruler
- 1 (46", 2mm) silver finish cable chain
- 1 (12mm) silver finish lobster clasp

1 Begin with the 4-sided pewter blank, which is stampable on all of the 4 sides; have one of the two sides without the hole facing you. For these slim blanks, much like stamping on washers, you will not need to use Stamp Straight Tape. Instead, tape the blank to the block only to secure it from moving as you stamp. Rather than use the tape to guide your stamping, you'll look down on your stamp and make sure it's centered vertically on the blank, and not hanging off over the top or bottom edge of the blank. Don't be nervous about not having your tape as your safety net! Slim blanks and washers can often be easier to stamp than larger areas, as long as you take your time when placing each stamp. Your message, "adventure awaits," should be stamped on a side of the blank without a hole at the top, and placing the tape close to the bottom of the blank will allow you to easily begin your message.

2 When you finish the word "adventure," move your tape so that you can continue stamping the second word, "awaits." You can place the tape over the previously stamped letters to hold the blank steady as you continue. Finally, if you have additional room remaining on the blank, stamp a 3mm heart stamp, or your favorite 3mm design stamp, to finish off the piece.

3   Apply the enamel by squirting a few lines directly onto your piece. Rub in the enamel with a paper towel, making sure it gets all the way into your impressions; wait 10 seconds, then polish it clean. Continue to wipe the piece gently until the surface is cleaned of any enamel, and all that remains are the darkened impressions. If you find that you've accidentally wiped it out of the impressions, you can re-apply it and try again. If this happens, try waiting a few seconds longer the second time before wiping the enamel away.

4   Next, you'll create the beaded charm for your second chain. Slide the beads onto a 2" jewelry head pin, beginning with the 2mm bead and then adding the tube bead. Grip the head pin just above the beads with your round nose pliers, and wrap the wire end of the head pin around one side of your pliers, forming a loop.

5   Now take the wire end and wrap it around the head pin under the loop you created. Wrap it in neat coils around the wire until the space between the loop and the top of the bead has been filled. There's no minimum number of wraps for your charm to be secure; as long as it wraps around just once, it will be strong enough to hold up to regular wear. Additional wraps are just to fill the gap instead of allowing the bead to slide around.

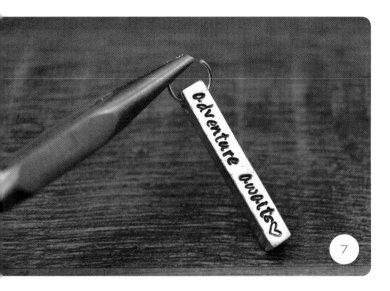

6   If there's any excess wire when you're done wrapping it, trim it off with wire cutters. Note: take caution when cutting small pieces of wire; they don't always drop to the table and may fly into the air. Ensure you collect and dispose of all remnant pieces. If any bit of wire is sticking out that may catch on clothing after you've trimmed it, press it down with your chain nose pliers so that it wraps snugly around the base of the head pin.

7   Because of the placement of the hole in the blank, a large jump ring will need to be added before stringing the charm. Twist open the 12mm jump ring with your chain nose pliers by using two sets of pliers to grab on either side of the seam in the ring. Twist the pliers and ends of the jump ring away from each other in a north-south motion. Slide the stamped metal blank onto the jump ring, then close the ring by twisting the ends back toward each other so the ends of the ring are flush. Now, add a 7mm jump ring to the initial 12mm ring, and a second 7mm jump ring to the loop of your bead charm so that you can string your pendants onto each segment of chain in the following step.

8   Measure 20" along the chain, and add a 7mm
    jump ring through one of the links of the cable
    chain at that point, following the process you did
    in the last step to open and close a jump ring.
    This will create two chains leading off the ring
    that measure 20" and 26". For ease of wear, add
    a second jump ring attached to the first ring, so
    that there are two connected rings at the 20"
    point.

9   String the beaded charm onto the shorter chain,
    and the stamped bar onto the longer chain.
    Finally, take the two ends of the chain and
    connect them together with a final jump ring.
    Add the lobster clasp to this ring before twisting
    it closed to finish your necklace. ●

#stampinghacks

If you prefer to work with a flat blank, then not
to worry—any slim rectangular blank can be
substituted in this design, as long as it's 1½" or
longer. And if you end up with too much space
before, after, or between words—try adding a
simple design stamp to fill the space. It will
balance the piece and look totally natural!

Bright Ideas Necklace

DIY STAMPED METAL JEWELRY

YOU'VE BEEN KNOWN to have a bright idea every so often, right? Show off your inner genius with this playful two-finish piece. By incorporating an uncommon artisan blank into this design, you can make a beautiful necklace (and a proud statement) with even the most basic of stamping skills. A quick search online for artisan stamping blanks will bring up a lot of choices outside the typical circles, rectangles, and hearts. Now that stamping is a popular passion, the available supplies are becoming increasingly innovative! Let the metal work for you with this bright idea.

materials

- 1 (¾") bronze spiral pendant blank
- Steel block
- Stamp Straight Tape or washi tape
- 2.5mm ImpressArt Scarlett's Signature font alphabet stamps, or 2.5mm alphabet stamps in font of your choice, in uppercase
- Stamping hammer
- 3mm star design stamp
- Awl (optional)

- 1 (⅝") round aluminum tag
- 6mm light bulb design stamp
- Stamp enamel
- Paper towel
- 1 (7mm) silver finish jump ring
- Chain nose pliers
- 1 (18", 2mm) gold finish necklace chain with clasp

1 Because this spiral pendant comes with the bail—the top loop that will string onto your necklace—already soldered on, this blank will need to be stamped on the edge of your steel block. Tape it down to secure it, and just like you learned for designs involving round washers and slim blanks in the Unicorn Magic Necklace and Adventurer's Double-Pendant Necklace earlier in this chapter, you'll let the shape of the blank guide your letters instead of using tape to stamp your message straight. This message is intended to be read at the top of the spiral, so you'll be stamping at the top of the piece. Rotate your steel block so the first letter you want to stamp is straight ahead, and position the stamp so that it faces you. Before you strike, ensure that the stamp is centered vertically on the blank and that it isn't hanging over the top or bottom edge.

2 Stamp your message, "CREATIVE GENIUS," along the top edge of the spiral, continuing to rotate your steel block as you go to easily stamp in a spiral, moving your tape as needed. You can also add decorative stamps and dots to give it a whimsical look. The addition of a star and a few dots made with a standard awl (just place and tap the top of the awl with your hammer very gently, as you would do for a letter or design stamp) will give the spiral a celestial feel.

3   On your small round aluminum tag, place the light bulb stamp directly in the center. Check around the edges of the stamp to be sure it's centered on the blank. Large design stamps will be easier to hold flat and not tilted in any direction, because the surface area of the design is larger. Because we'll be stamping a more intricate design and displacing more metal, though, you'll need to use more force when you strike the stamp with your hammer than you use for your smaller letter stamps.

4   Apply the enamel by squirting a few lines directly onto your pieces. Rub in the enamel with a paper towel, making sure it gets all the way into your impressions; wait 10 seconds, then polish the pieces clean. Continue to wipe the pieces gently until the surfaces are cleaned of any enamel, and all that remains are the darkened impressions. If you find that you've accidentally wiped it out of the impressions, you can re-apply it and try again. If this happens, try waiting a few seconds longer the second time before wiping the enamel away.

5   Twist open a 7mm jump ring with your chain nose pliers by using two sets of pliers to grab on either side of the seam in the ring. Twist the pliers and ends of the jump ring away from each other in a north-south motion. Slide on the round light bulb tag and twist the jump ring closed again, completing your light bulb charm. String both charms onto a coordinated necklace chain to finish your brilliant piece. ●

#stampinghacks

Spirals are very forgiving if you can't manage to center your words perfectly. Choose the edge where you wish to begin, and rotate your steel block as you go, so that the first letter you want to stamp is straight ahead, and position the stamp so that it faces you exactly. Before you strike it, take a moment to ensure that the stamp is centered vertically on the blank, and that the stamp isn't hanging over the top or the bottom edge.

Love Bites Puff Pendant

WHETHER YOU'VE BEEN through a rough patch or a breakup, or you can't find a great date, sometimes . . . love bites. It's a fact of life! This little puff pendant is a great piece for expressing yourself when things aren't going your way in the romance department. Coupled with a pint of ice cream, it's also a great gift when a girlfriend needs a pep talk!

materials

- 1 (½") copper circle blank
- Steel block
- Stamp Straight Tape or washi tape
- Pen or fine-tip marker
- 4mm ImpressArt Lollipop font alphabet stamps, or 4mm alphabet stamps in font of your choice, in uppercase
- Stamping hammer
- Stamp enamel
- Paper towel
- Doming block and punch
- Heavy-duty adhesive (like E6000)
- 1 (¾") bezel pendant with ½" well
- 1 (7mm) silver finish jump ring
- Chain nose pliers
- 1 (18", 2mm) silver finish necklace chain with clasp

1 Adhere your copper blank to your steel block with Stamp Straight Tape, placing it where the bottom of each of the four letters will be stamped on the first line, just above the center of your blank. Use your pen or fine-tip marker to mark off the placement of your letters. Stamp the word "LOVE," then remove the tape. Move the Stamp Straight Tape down to the second line, directly underneath the first word, marking five letters on the tape. Stamp the word "BITES" and remove the tape again.

2 Apply the enamel by squirting a few lines directly onto your piece. Rub in the enamel with a paper towel, making sure it gets all the way into your impressions; wait 10 seconds, then polish it clean. Continue to wipe the piece gently until the surface is cleaned of any enamel, and all that remains are the darkened impressions. If you find that you've accidentally wiped it out of the impressions, you can re-apply it and try again. If this happens, try waiting a few seconds longer the second time before wiping the enamel away.

3 To prevent your blank from getting scratched during the doming process, cover the stamped side with a piece of tape. Place the copper blank, stamped side down, into the deepest well of the doming block. Position the punch on the back side of the blank, and tap the top of the punch with your hammer several times. Move the blank around and be sure to apply the punch to the full area of the copper circle. If you notice that it's not evenly domed, you can go back and continue doming.

DIY STAMPED METAL JEWELRY

4 When you're happy with the result, add heavy-duty adhesive to the inside of the bezel well, making sure to apply it around the corners of the bezel walls especially, where you'll be gluing the domed copper disc into place. Add the disc to the bezel, taking care to align it with the bail at the top of the bezel. Allow it to dry fully, which can take anywhere from a few hours to overnight.

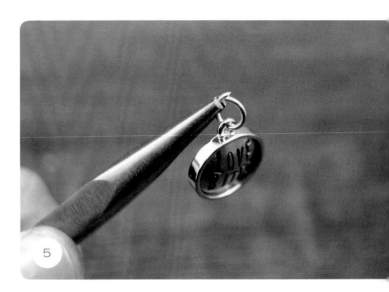

5 Finish your necklace by attaching a jump ring to the bail—twist open the 7mm jump ring with your chain nose pliers by using two sets of pliers to grab on either side of the seam in the ring. Twist the pliers and ends of the jump ring away from each other in a north-south motion. Add the charm to the jump ring, then close the ring by twisting the ends back toward each other so the ends of the ring are flush. String the puffy charm onto an 18" necklace chain with clasp, and step out in style! ●

Be Wild Layered Necklace

THIS DOUBLE-DISC NECKLACE sports a tangle of wildflowers—because sometimes it's good to be wild! The floral theme gives this piece a sweet appearance, but we all know you've got to watch the wild ones for an occasional thorn, and the message here has just enough flair to send a bold statement. The pinch bail called for in this project gives personality to your piece and is easy to use. Notice how the leaf-shaped bail shown in the project photos enhances the theme of a wild garden!

materials

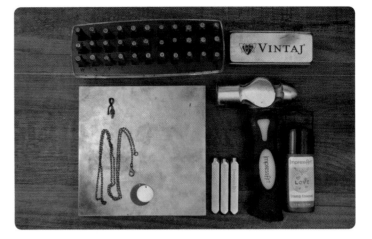

- 25mm round brass blank, treated with patina
- Stamp Straight Tape or washi tape
- Steel block
- 6mm flower design stamp
- Stamping hammer
- 3mm flower design stamp
- Buffing pad or buffing block
- Nylon hammer
- ¾" round aluminum blank
- 3mm ImpressArt Bridgette font alphabet stamps, or 3mm alphabet stamps in font of your choice, in lowercase

- 6mm leaf or vine design stamp
- Stamp enamel
- Paper towel
- Floral- or leaf-themed brass finish pinch bail
- Chain nose pliers
- 1 (18", 2mm) brass necklace chain with clasp

1 Prepare your round brass blank by taping it to your steel block, just to keep it from shifting as you stamp. Stamp it all over with a 6mm floral design stamp. As you fill the blank with flowers, move the tape periodically so that the entire circle is covered with the design stamp. Then fill in the blank space left behind with a smaller 3mm flower design stamp.

2 Gently buff the stamped disc with the buffing pad or buffing block to bring a little shine back, and to add some light contrast to the flowers. You may also need to flatten the blank back out after stamping, using your nylon hammer; to do so, simply turn the blank face down on your steel block and hammer the back side until it's flat again. Thin blanks tend to curl the more you stamp on the front side.

3 Next, tape your aluminum blank to your block near the top of the circle, leaving the lower part free to stamp your message. Begin by stamping your words, "be wild." To stamp along the bottom of a disc, carefully align the stamp with the outer edge of the disc by looking down from the top of the stamp. The edge of the stamp that faces you should be placed level with the edge of the blank. After stamping the message, use your design stamps in the area above to add a few vines or leaves around the edges, with a tangle of flowers in the center. Don't worry about even stamping and spacing! Because we're going for a wild theme, this is a great time to practice using larger design stamps.

DIY STAMPED METAL JEWELRY

4 Apply the enamel by squirting a few lines directly onto your piece. Rub in the enamel with a paper towel, making sure it gets all the way into your impressions; wait 10 seconds, then polish it clean. Continue to wipe the piece gently until the surface is cleaned of any enamel, and all that remains are the darkened impressions. If you find that you've accidentally wiped it out of the impressions, you can re-apply it and try again. If this happens, try waiting a few seconds longer the second time before wiping the enamel away.

5 Align the pegs on the inside of the bail with the holes in your round blanks, stacking first the larger brass blank and then the smaller aluminum blank on top. Pinch the bail closed with chain nose pliers.

6 String your pendant onto an 18" brass necklace chain with clasp to finish the necklace, and enjoy this design any time you're feeling a little bit bold! ●

#stampinghacks

Background textures are a great way to get familiar with design stamps! When working with larger stamps, you have to displace more metal to get a clean and even impression. You often have to strike quite a bit harder on large stamps to get the look you want.

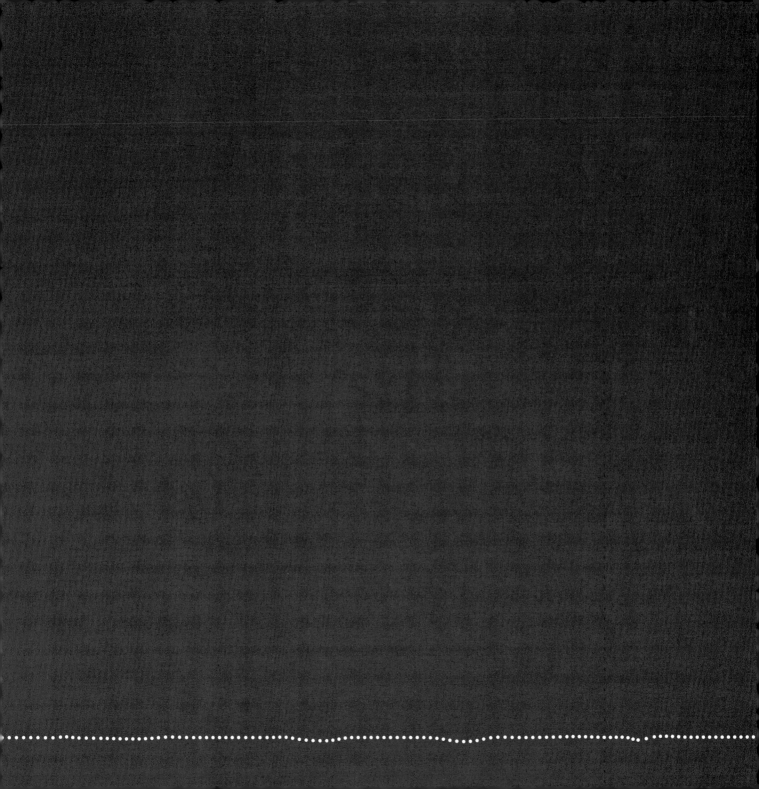

CHAPTER 4

Bracelets

My love of bracelets began on the school playground, where I was pretty much the queen of friendship bracelets. Creating gifts for people I care about is a pleasure that has stayed with me all these years, making bracelets the most meaningful pieces of jewelry in my collection—and you'll even find a nod to the classic friendship bracelet in the coming chapter.

Whether you've got a boho style and love leather and fibers or you prefer the polished look of beads and charms, there are designs in this chapter for everyone. Express yourself and your style with the inspirational Fearless Leather Cuff or the playful Flirty Charm Bangles or with other projects, all ranging from beginner to intermediate. Get colorful—and get stamping!—with these great bracelet ideas.

Flirty Charm
Bangles

THESE STACKABLE CHARM bangles are great wrist candy, and they tell the world all about the real you. Are you Flirty? Sassy? Smart? Happy? Faithful? These days, design stamps are available to reflect nearly every hobby and passion. Personalize tiny discs with your initials, your favorite designs, and words to inspire you or show off your style. They're best worn in multiples, and this project yields 3 bracelets, so there's room to say plenty about yourself!

materials

- 2 (9mm) copper disc blanks
- 2 (9mm) silver disc blanks
- 1 (12mm) silver finish pewter disc blank
- 1 (12mm) gold finish pewter disc blank
- Steel block
- Stamp Straight Tape or washi tape
- Pen or fine-tip marker
- 3mm heart and star design stamps
- 3mm ImpressArt Bridgette font alphabet stamps, or 3mm alphabet stamps of your choice, in upper- and lowercase

- Stamping hammer
- Stamp enamel
- Paper towel
- 2 (4mm) crystal beads
- 3 (6mm) crystal beads
- 5 (2") silver finish jewelry head pins
- Round nose pliers
- Wire cutters
- Chain nose pliers
- 11 (7mm) silver finish jump rings
- 3 silver finish adjustable wire bangle bracelets

1 For each charm bangle you make, stamp two charms. Tape all of your blanks to the steel block to hold them steady as you work. Stamp one copper blank with a heart in the center, another copper blank with a star in the center, one silver blank with the initial "A," and one more silver blank with the lucky number 55.

2 Adhere your first pewter blank to your steel block with Stamp Straight Tape, placing it where the bottom of each letter will be stamped on the first line of the message, "sassy girl." Use your pen or fine-tip marker to mark off the placement of your letters. Stamp the letters "s," "a," "s," and the final "s," and then remove the tape. Replace the Stamp Straight Tape, lining up the bottom of the tape with the tops of the stamped letters. Place the letter "y" so that the top of the letter stamp rests against the bottom of the tape, and stamp the final letter. (This technique of filling in descending letters should be familiar to you if you created the "Quote of the Day" Cuff Bracelet in Chapter 2.)

3 Remove the tape again, placing it at the bottom of the lower line of text, "girl." Stamp the letters "i," "r," and "l," move the tape just as you did for the "y" in the previous line, and stamp the final letter to complete the message.

#happystamping

These 9mm copper and silver blanks are the perfect size for 1–2 impressions, so stamp designs, monograms, and lucky numbers on this size blank. The 12mm blanks can fit more characters, so short names and messages fit well.

4   The second pewter blank features the word "FLIRT." Place your Stamp Straight Tape and mark your letters for this blank just as you did for the first 12mm blank, and stamp your word. Then, move your tape down to align where you want a heart to go below your word. Stamp your heart.

5   Apply the enamel to each blank by squirting a few lines directly onto each piece. Rub in the enamel with a paper towel, making sure it gets all the way into your impressions; wait 10 seconds, then polish it clean. Continue to wipe the piece gently until the surface is cleaned of any enamel, and all that remains are the darkened impressions. If you find that you've accidentally wiped it out of the impressions, you can re-apply it and try again. If this happens, try waiting a few seconds longer the second time before wiping the enamel away. Repeat this process for each charm until all your impressions have been darkened.

6   Next, create beaded charms by adding a bead onto a 2" jewelry head pin. Grip the head pin just above the bead with your round nose pliers, and wrap the wire end of the head pin around one side of your pliers, forming a loop.

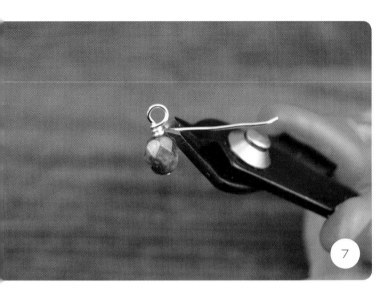

7   Next, take the wire end of the pin and wrap it around the base of the head pin under the loop you created. Wrap it in neat coils around the wire until the space between the loop and the top of the bead has been filled. There's no minimum number of wraps for your charm to be secure; as long as it wraps around just once, it will be strong enough to hold up to regular wear. Additional wraps are just to fill the gap instead of allowing the bead to slide around. If there's any excess wire when you're done wrapping it, trim it off with wire cutters. Note: take caution when cutting small pieces of wire; they don't always drop to the table and may fly into the air. Ensure you collect and dispose of all remnant pieces. If any bit of wire is sticking out that may catch on clothing after you've trimmed it, press it down with your chain nose pliers so that it wraps snugly around the base of the head pin.

8   Twist open a 7mm jump ring with your chain nose pliers by using two sets of pliers to grab on either side of the seam in the ring. Twist the pliers and ends of the jump ring away from each other in a north-south motion. Slide the charm onto the jump ring, then close the ring by twisting the ends back toward each other so the ends of the ring are flush. Repeat until all blanks and beaded charms have been attached to jump rings.

9   Slip the jump rings with the attached charms onto your bangles, adding 2 stamped charms and 1–2 beaded charms onto each bracelet. Stack them, wear them, love them—they're perfect for expressing yourself! ●

Friends Are Rock Stars
Friendship Bracelets

materials

THERE'S SOMETHING ABOUT tying on a gift from a friend that appeals to the kid in all of us. This bracelet makes up in no time at all, and you can stamp it with names, inside jokes, or something inspirational. It will always remind your besties of the fun times you've spent together!

- 1 (1") brass oval connector blank

- Steel block

- Stamp Straight Tape or washi tape

- Pen or fine-tip marker

- 4mm ImpressArt Lollipop font alphabet stamps, or 3–4mm alphabet stamps in font of your choice, in uppercase

- 3mm ImpressArt Solid Star Design Stamp, or 3mm design stamp of your choice

- Stamping hammer

- 2 (1") copper oval connector blanks

- Stamp enamel

- Paper towel

- Bracelet bending pliers

- 60" of 20 lb. hemp twine or cord for each bracelet

1 Adhere your brass blank to your steel block with Stamp Straight Tape, placing it where the bottom of each letter will be stamped. Use your pen or fine-tip marker to mark off the placement of your letters for the message, "ROCK STAR." Stamp your message on the blank, and fill the gap between the words with a 3mm star stamp to suit the theme. One-inch blanks are not very wide; your message will fill the blank from one edge to the other. Repeat this process, stamping "WRITER," "MAKER," or your own personal message, on the copper blanks. Surround these smaller words with one star on both the left and right sides of the word, to fill the blank completely.

2 Apply the enamel to each blank by squirting a few lines directly onto each piece. Rub in the enamel with a paper towel, making sure it gets all the way into your impressions; wait 10 seconds, then polish it clean. Continue to wipe the piece gently until the surface is cleaned of any enamel, and all that remains are the darkened impressions. If you find that you've accidentally wiped it out of the impressions, you can re-apply it and try again. If this happens, try waiting a few seconds longer the second time before wiping the enamel away.

3 These thin blanks are likely to curl a bit when you stamp them. You can correct this curling with bracelet bending pliers. Place the blank between the nylon pads of the pliers, with the letters facing the concave side of the pliers and the back side facing the convex side, and squeeze the two sides together to bend the metal blank. This will curve the blank so that it rests nicely against the wrist, with the letters facing outward.

4   For each bracelet, cut one 60" length of hemp twine into 3 lengths measuring 20" each. Thread one strand through the hole on one side of the stamped blank and the second strand through the hole on the other side of the blank, so that you will have a 10" doubled string coming from each side of the bracelet.

5   Place the third strand of hemp twine behind your stamped blank, and align it with the other two strings on each side. These three strings can now be braided together. On one side, braid for a length of 3½" to 4", and tie an overhand knot to secure the braid. Turn the bracelet around, and repeat the process on the opposite side. Your finished bracelet will have one cord that runs behind the stamped blank, but it won't show. This cord strengthens the point where the cord connects to the metal blank, extending the life of your bracelet.

6   Trim the tails so that they are even, leaving them long. Remember, your friends will need the tails when they tie them on for some old-school fun! ●

#stampinghacks

Haven't invested in bracelet bending pliers? You can shape small blanks by pressing them against something round, like a cup, a roll of tape, or a can. Not sure you can commit to tying on a bracelet permanently? Modify this design by adding glue-on end clasps to each end for an easily removable version!

Til Death Bead Bangles

materials

NOT EVERYONE IS a gushy person when it comes to love. Love is a wonderful thing, but life isn't a romantic comedy, with everyone goggle-eyed over the idea. If you're of the same mind (or have a great friend getting married who is), then this cheeky, gothic-inspired take on some Mr. and Mrs. jewelry will suit perfectly.

- Steel block
- 3 (½") pewter cube beads
- 4mm ImpressArt Lollipop font alphabet stamps, or other 3–4mm slim font alphabet stamps of your choice
- 3mm heart stamp
- 6mm skull and crossbones stamp
- Stamping hammer
- Stamp enamel
- Paper towel
- 3 ball closure wire bangle bracelets
- 6 (9mm) large-hole beads
- 2 (12mm) large-hole beads

1   You will be free-stamping these cubes, meaning you won't need Stamp Straight Tape at all. To center your letters, note the position of the stamp in relation to the top and bottom edges of the cube as you look down the top of the stamp. Do your best to keep the stamp centered between the top and bottom edges. On the first cube, stamp "TIL" on any of the 4 sides. Turn the cube, and stamp a heart design, centering in the middle of the blank. Rotate again and stamp "MR." Rotate it one last time to stamp the final side, and stamp another heart.

2   For the second cube, begin by stamping the skull and crossbones in the center of the cube. Rotate the cube and stamp the word "LOVE." Rotate it again and stamp the word "AND." Rotate it to the final side and stamp a heart design, centered in the middle of the face of the cube.

3   On the final cube, stamp "DEATH" on one face of the cube. Rotate it and stamp a heart in the center. Rotate it a third time, stamping "MRS," and on the final side, stamp another centered heart.

4   When you've stamped your messages, apply the
    enamel to each cube by squirting a few lines
    directly onto each piece. Rub in the enamel with
    a paper towel, making sure it gets all the way
    into your impressions; wait 10 seconds, then
    polish it clean. Continue to wipe the piece gently
    until the surface is cleaned of any enamel, and
    all that remains are the darkened impressions.
    If you find that you've accidentally wiped it out
    of the impressions, you can re-apply it and try
    again. If this happens, try waiting a few seconds
    longer the second time before wiping the enamel
    away.

5   Unscrew the ball closure on your bangle
    bracelet, and add a 9mm bead and then your
    cubes, ensuring that the messages read in the
    correct order from left to right—for example
    "MR AND MRS" on one combination. Finish the
    bangle with another 9mm bead. The cubes will
    rotate freely, so you won't always see the same
    messages, making this a fun mix-and-match
    piece! Add additional bead bangles to stack
    with your stamped bangle with a 12mm bead
    surrounded by a pair of 9mm beads. For the
    right friend, adding your messages and using
    her wedding colors would make for a great bridal
    shower gift—or sport your own marital pride
    anytime you like. ●

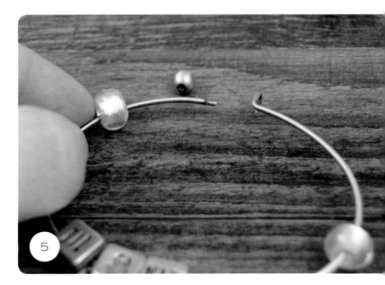

On Fire Leather Bracelet

DIY STAMPED METAL JEWELRY

ARE YOU A little too hot to handle sometimes? Tell the world you're on fire with this subtly designed layered leather bracelet. Layers of leather give you the look of stacked or wrapped bracelets without any tangles, so you can still pair them with other arm candy, and store them in your jewelry box easily among your other pieces!

materials

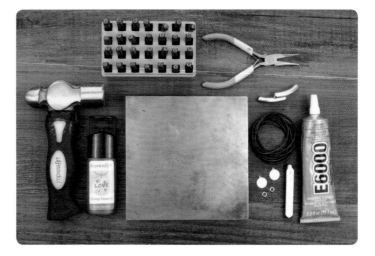

- 2 (½") aluminum or silver round tag-shaped blanks
- Steel block
- Stamp Straight Tape or washi tape
- Pen or fine-tip marker
- 3mm ImpressArt Newsprint font alphabet stamps, or 3mm alphabet stamps in font of your choice, in lowercase
- 6mm fire design stamp
- Stamping hammer
- Stamp enamel

- Paper towel
- 32" (2mm) leather cord, cut into 4 (8") pieces
- Glue-on end clasp with a 5–6mm opening
- Heavy-duty adhesive (like E6000)
- 2 (7mm) silver finish jump rings
- Chain nose pliers
- 6 (6mm) large-hole silver beads (at least 2mm hole)

1. Adhere your first blank to your steel block with Stamp Straight Tape, placing it where the bottom of each of the two letters will be stamped on the first line. Use your pen or fine-tip marker to mark off the placement of your letters. Stamp the word "on," then remove the tape. Move the Stamp Straight Tape down to the second line, marking four letters on the tape. Stamp the word "fire" and remove the tape again.

2. On your second blank, tape the tag's ring to the block to hold it steady, and center the fire design stamp on the circle. Strike the design stamp with more force than you would for your letter stamps, as there is more metal to displace to get a crisp impression.

3. Apply the enamel to each blank by squirting a few lines directly onto each piece. Rub in the enamel with a paper towel, making sure it gets all the way into your impressions; wait 10 seconds, then polish it clean. Continue to wipe the piece gently until the surface is cleaned of any enamel, and all that remains are the darkened impressions. If you find that you've accidentally wiped it out of the impressions, you can re-apply it and try again. If this happens, try waiting a few seconds longer the second time before wiping the enamel away.

4 Gather all 4 of your cords, and glue them into one end of your clasp with heavy-duty adhesive. Set aside and allow the glue to dry until tacky, or the cords do not pull easily away from the clasp when gently tugged. Work gently on the following steps so as not to pull the cords loose before the glue dries.

5 Attach the 7mm jump rings to the stamped blanks by twisting them with your chain nose pliers by using two sets of pliers to grab on either side of the seam in the ring. Twist the pliers and ends of the jump rings away from each other in a north-south motion. Add the tag, then close the rings by twisting the ends back toward each other so the ends of the ring are flush.

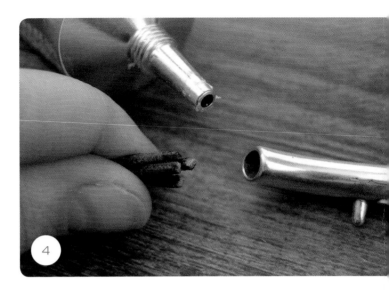

6 Next, add the large-hole beads to your design, threading 1–2 beads directly onto each leather cord. When looking for beads large enough to use with leather, try shopping in the section that sells leather cord.

7 The final step will vary based on the size of your end clasp, just as in the Untamed Leather Bracelet in Chapter 2. Be sure to adjust the length of your leather depending on the size of your clasp. Measure the length of the clasp past where the leather will be glued in. Cut your leather bracelet to a length of 6½". Glue the leather cord, with beads and stamped charm slid on, into the wells of the clasp and let dry according to package directions. ●

I Sparkle Beaded Bracelet

DO YOU HAVE a sparkling personality? Of course you do! And you don't have to justify it to anyone! I love a bold statement coming from a woman of confidence, and this beaded bracelet delivers. Layers of chain fill out this bracelet, giving you a stacked look with just one piece. Try this design with different styles of chain to give it a totally different look and feel.

materials

- 1½" pewter oval blank with 2 holes
- Steel block
- Stamp Straight Tape or washi tape
- Pen or fine-tip marker
- 4mm ImpressArt Lollipop font alphabet stamps, or 3–4mm alphabet stamps in font of your choice, in uppercase
- 4mm ImpressArt Star Design Stamp included in the Lollipop font alphabet stamp set, or 4mm design stamp of your choice

- Stamping hammer
- Awl
- Stamp enamel
- Paper towel
- Bracelet bending pliers
- 23" (2mm) beaded link chain
- Chain nose pliers
- 6 (6mm) jump rings
- 3 (15mm) jump rings
- S-hook clasp

1 Adhere your pewter blank to your steel block with Stamp Straight Tape, placing it where the bottom of each letter will be stamped for the top row of text, "BECAUSE I SPARKLE." Stamp Straight Tape can be placed in a curve; it is just flexible enough that it can be placed in a gentle arc like this oval. Use your pen or fine-tip marker to mark off the placement of your letters, then stamp the first line of the message. Remove the tape, and place it along the bottom of the blank, curving it slightly to follow the bottom arc, and mark the second line of text, "THAT'S WHY." Stamp these letters along the bottom of the blank.

2 To emphasize your sparkle and to fill the space in the middle of the blank, stamp a few stars! Add a row of 3 stars in the center of the oval, between the top and bottom lines of text. To add a stardust effect around stars, as shown, use an awl for precise placement. Just set the tip exactly where you'd like a dot to appear, and tap the top of the awl very gently with your hammer.

3 Apply the enamel by squirting a few lines directly onto your piece. Rub in the enamel with a paper towel, making sure it gets all the way into your impressions; wait 10 seconds, then polish it clean. Continue to wipe the piece gently until the surface is cleaned of any enamel, and all that remains are the darkened impressions. If you find that you've accidentally wiped it out of the impressions, you can re-apply it and try again. If this happens, try waiting a few seconds longer the second time before wiping the enamel away.

4 Curve the blank to fit your wrist by pressing it with bracelet bending pliers, with the letters facing outward.

5 Cut or twist open the links of your beaded chain to separate it into 6 lengths: 4 that are 2½" in length, and 2 that are 6½" in length. Twist open a 6mm jump ring with your chain nose pliers by using two sets of pliers to grab on either side of the seam in the ring. Twist the pliers and ends of the jump ring away from each other in a north-south motion. Slide the last link of both of the two shorter lengths of chain onto the jump ring, then close the ring by twisting the ends back toward each other so the ends of the ring are flush. Repeat this process with the other two short lengths of chain to attach them to one jump ring.

6 Next, connect these short chains to your stamped oval using another 6mm jump ring on each side, connected from the first jump ring (from step 5) to the oval itself. You should now have two strands of chain attached to your center oval on each side.

7 On each end of the bracelet, twist open a 15mm jump ring. Add four chains from one side to this large ring, and close it. Repeat this process on the other side, so that 2 short chains go from each side to the clasp and 2 long chains go from one side of the clasp to the other across the back of your blank. All that's left to complete the bracelet is to attach a clasp and ring to the ends, so with your remaining small jump rings, attach the S-hook to one end, squeezing the clasp closed, and a large ring to the opposite side for the hook to clasp onto. ●

Fearless Leather Cuff

THIS BRACELET WILL show you how to use rivets in your work to attach stamped and textured metals directly to leather for a great mixed media look. This cuff's butterfly theme adds a hint of femininity, while the leather gives you a rugged appeal. If you're not afraid, then try your hand at this fearless design!

materials

- Screw-down hole punch with ³⁄₃₂" hole
- Pen or fine-tip marker
- 1 (1½") rectangle pewter blank
- Steel block
- Stamp Straight Tape or washi tape
- 3mm ImpressArt Newsprint font alphabet stamps, or 3mm alphabet stamps in font of your choice, in uppercase
- Stamping hammer
- Stamp enamel
- Paper towel
- 1 (1¾") brass butterfly blank, treated with patina
- Wire cutters
- Metal file
- Buffing pad or buffing block
- Bracelet bending pliers
- 1" wide leather cuff with snap
- ³⁄₃₂" leather punch or awl
- 4 (4mm) compression rivets
- Rivet-setting tool

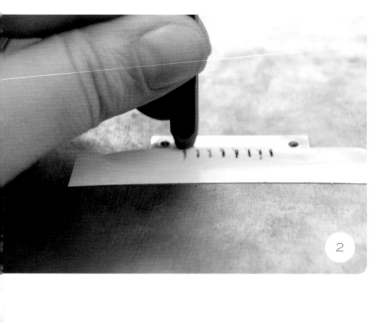

1 First, if your rectangle blank doesn't already have two holes, you'll need to punch a second ³⁄₃₂" hole in the opposite side, so that you can rivet it onto the leather cuff. With a fine-tip marker or a gentle tap of your awl, plan the placement of the hole so that it is balanced with the existing hole. Then slip the blank under the ³⁄₃₂" side of your screw-down punch, and twist the punch until it presses a hole through the metal.

2 Adhere your pewter blank to your steel block with Stamp Straight Tape, placing it where the bottom of each letter will be stamped. Use your pen or fine-tip marker to mark off the placement of your letters, then stamp the word "FEARLESS."

3 Apply the enamel by squirting a few lines directly onto your piece. Rub in the enamel with a paper towel, making sure it gets all the way into your impressions; wait 10 seconds, then polish it clean. Continue to wipe the piece gently until the surface is cleaned of any enamel, and all that remains are the darkened impressions. If you find that you've accidentally wiped it out of the impressions, you can re-apply it and try again. If this happens, try waiting a few seconds longer the second time before wiping the enamel away.

4 Next, prepare the butterfly blank. Because the holes are too small to accommodate rivets, use wire cutters to snip off the rings on each side, and use a metal file to smooth away any sharp corners that may be left behind from making these small cuts. Punch ³⁄₃₂" holes in the upper part of each wing, as shown.

5 Texturize your butterfly by hammering it with the round end of your hammer, until there are no smooth areas remaining on the butterfly blank. Buff it with the buffing pad or buffing block to create contrast and bring out the shine.

6 Press your blanks with bracelet bending pliers to curve them, so they sit nicely on the wrist.

7 Line up your blanks on the leather cuff, and using a leather punch or an awl, create small (³⁄₃₂") holes in the leather cuff where the rivets will be set. Press the flat back side of the rivet through the back of the leather, place the stamped metal blank on top of both the flat side of the rivet and leather, stacking it onto the exposed core of the rivet, and snap the rounded cap into place on top.

8 Position the cuff on your steel block with the flat side of the rivet facing down. Use the curved end of your rivet-setting tool to set the rivet by tapping it firmly with your hammer several times. When it doesn't twist or wiggle, it's set. Rivet first the butterfly and then the rectangle bar onto the cuff, the bar overlapping the butterfly blank. ●

#happystamping

Instead of a butterfly in the background, you can use other brass shapes to change the look and feel of this piece. It becomes a great unisex piece by using geometric shapes like circles or ovals in the background!

Butterfly Bangle Bracelet

THIS DESIGN IS a bit different in that we aren't starting with a bracelet base, but rather creating our own. The butterflies lie diagonally, attached at the top of one wing and the bottom of the next butterfly. Butterflies have long been a symbol of change and transformation. Things can get awfully comfortable in our cocoons sometimes, but great things happen when we bust out and spread our wings. Wearing a butterfly is a great reminder that sometimes we're destined to be even more amazing than we already are.

materials

- 5 (1⁵⁄₁₆") copper butterfly blanks
- 4 (1⁵⁄₁₆") nickel silver butterfly blanks
- Steel block
- Stamp Straight Tape or washi tape
- Fine-tip marker
- 3mm ImpressArt Newsprint font alphabet stamps, or 3mm alphabet stamps in font of your choice, in lowercase
- Spiral and floral design stamps
- Stamping hammer
- Screw-down hole punch with ³⁄₃₂" hole
- Ruler (optional)
- Stamp enamel
- Paper towel
- Metal patinas—marine and verdigris (optional)
- Sponge paintbrush (optional)
- Bracelet bending pliers
- 9 (4mm) compression rivets
- Rivet-setting tool
- Buffing pad or buffing block (optional)

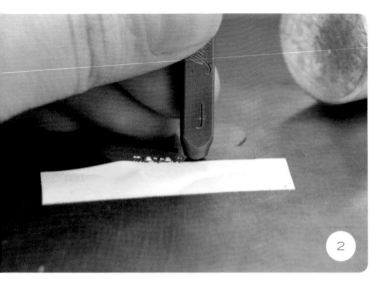

1 Angle the butterfly blank so that the level center of the text will run from the top of the left wing to the lower part of the right wing. Adhere each blank to your steel block with the tape, placing it where the bottom of each letter will be stamped. Alternating between copper and silver blanks, plan out your message, "never fear changes for they can be amazing." Two copper blanks will rest side by side when all the blanks are finally attached together, because there is an odd number of blanks.

2 Begin by marking the letter placement for the words "never fear" on the first blank, "changes for" on the second, "they can be" on the third, and "amazing" on the fourth. Stamp these letters, skipping over the "g's" and the "y," and completing each of the other letters. As you encounter these lowercase letters with descenders, you will stamp them last. Remove the tape from below the letters, and replace it above the stamped letters, aligning the bottom of the tape with the tops of the short letters, such as "a" and "n." Place the "g" and the "y" stamps so that the top of the stamp aligns with the bottom of the tape, and finish the message on each blank. The remaining blanks should be stamped with an all-over pattern of flowers on the copper blanks and spirals on the silver blanks.

3 Punch a 3/32" hole on the top left wing and the lower right wing of each butterfly, aligning the holes level with your text. You can use a piece of Stamp Straight Tape or a ruler to aid in hole placement, if necessary. You can mark the spot to punch the hole with a fine-tip marker.

4 When you have one blank punched, use it as a template and mark on each butterfly with a fine-tip marker where to punch the holes so that they are all punched the same. You can see exactly where your holes will be if you look through the hole in the bottom of your screw-down punch.

5 Apply the enamel to each butterfly by squirting a few lines directly onto each piece. Rub in the enamel with a paper towel, making sure it gets all the way into your impressions; wait 10 seconds, then polish it clean. Continue to wipe the piece gently until the surface is cleaned of any enamel, and all that remains are the darkened impressions. If you find that you've accidentally wiped it out of the impressions, you can re-apply it and try again. If this happens, try waiting a few seconds longer the second time before wiping the enamel away. Repeat this process with the next blank once each blank is darkened.

6 Take a sponge brush and lightly dab coordinating colors of patina onto the edges of each blank.

7 Before you continue, allow your blanks to dry about 10 minutes, or until they are dry to the touch. Then use your bracelet bending pliers to curve each butterfly, aligning the holes in each blank with the edges of the pliers.

8 Rivet the butterflies together to form your bangle. Press the flat side of your rivet through the back side of the blanks, and snap the curved cap on top. Place the rivet flat side down on your steel block, and use the domed side of the rivet tool to set the rivet by tapping it firmly with your hammer several times. Take a moment to check that your blanks are aligned and the text is level before hammering the rivet all the way, because you won't be able to rotate the blanks after the rivets are set. After the blanks have been curved, you'll only be able to connect 2 or 3 of them together before moving on to another group of 2 or 3 blanks. Because of the curve of the butterflies, you will need to allow them to hang over the edges of your steel block, so the best place to do your riveting is on the corner of the steel block.

9 When you've connected as many butterflies as
   you can, you're ready to finish your piece and
   connect the groups of butterflies together to form
   a circle. After you've snapped the rivet into place
   between each group of blanks, place the bracelet
   curved side down on your steel block. Use the
   flat end of your rivet tool against the flat side of
   the rivet, and set it with your hammer. The rivets
   set backward like this will appear slightly flatter
   than the ones set the traditional way, but no
   one will notice, and it will secure your bracelet.
   Continue connecting butterflies together until
   you've formed a full circle, and let your finished
   bracelet be a reminder that without change,
   there would be no butterflies. ●

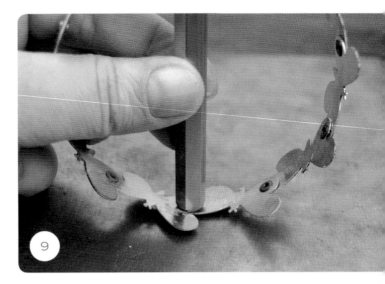

#happystamping

You can optionally experiment with patinas in
your favorite color scheme. To get the look shown
in this project, use a sponge brush and lightly
dab coordinating colors of patina onto the edges
of each blank—but there's no right or wrong way
to apply your patinas! This is a great variation
for customizing your own bracelet, adding as
much or as little color as you like. If you make
a mistake, you can wipe damp patina away with
a paper towel. If it begins to dry, it will need to
be buffed away with the buffing pad or buffing
block. You can always cover one color of patina
with another if you want to layer, change colors,
or cover something you don't like.

DIY STAMPED METAL JEWELRY

THIS TWIN-CHARM CUFF with a celestial theme is a twist on the traditional cuff, and it lies open at the top of the wrist. It's totally adjustable for the super star in your life, and it's even got a little bling for good measure! With this project, you'll learn how to safely set crystal rivets without cracking the gems.

materials

- 2 (⅝") circles of scrap craft vinyl
- 2 (⅞") aluminum circles
- Steel block
- Pen or fine-tip marker
- 3mm ImpressArt Bridgette font alphabet stamps, or 3mm alphabet stamps in font of your choice, in lowercase
- Stamping hammer
- 3mm star design stamp
- Awl

- Stamp enamel
- Paper towel
- Screw-down hole punch with ⅛" hole
- ¼" × 6" aluminum bracelet blank
- Bracelet bending pliers
- 2 (5mm) crystal compression rivets
- Rubber block
- Rivet-setting tool

1 Take your ⅝" circle of scrap craft vinyl and place it on the center of your aluminum circle blank as you stamp to help with your spacing, as Stamp Straight Tape does in your blanks with straight sides. This is the same technique used in the Hot Stuff Coffee Locket in Chapter 2 to help you when stamping in the round. Use your pen or fine-tip marker to mark off the placement of your letters for the message "shine on" on your first aluminum blank, and then stamp the letters to complete this phrase. On each side of the message, stamp a 3mm star, and then with your awl, gently tap three dots on each side of the star to resemble stardust.

2 On the second aluminum circle blank, place the vinyl circle on the center just as you did with the first, and mark the letter placement for the message "super star." Stamp these two words, and surround them with star stamps and dots to mirror your first disc.

3   Remove the vinyl, and apply the enamel by
    squirting a few lines directly onto your piece,
    darkening one disc at a time. Rub in the enamel
    with a paper towel, making sure it gets all the
    way into your impressions; wait 10 seconds, then
    polish it clean. Continue to wipe the piece gently
    until the surface is cleaned of any enamel, and
    all that remains are the darkened impressions.
    If you find that you've accidentally wiped it out
    of the impressions, you can re-apply it and try
    again. If this happens, try waiting a few seconds
    longer the second time before wiping the enamel
    away.

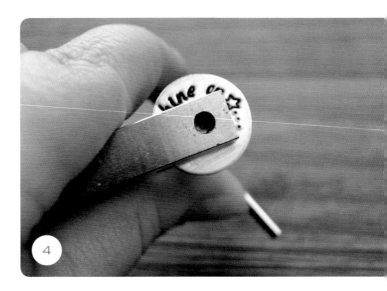

4   Mark the center of each blank with a fine-tip
    marker, and punch a ⅛" hole with your screw-
    down hole punch. Align the mark with the hole
    punch by checking the placement through the
    hole in the bottom of the punch. Screw the
    punch down until it pierces the metal, creating
    your hole. Punch a ⅛" hole, centered at each end
    of the bracelet blank as well.

5 Use your bracelet bending pliers to curve the cuff, pressing the strip between the nylon pads from one end to the other. Press each of the round charms with the pliers as well, aligning the center of the text with one edge of the pliers. You must curve them now; you would have trouble curving them after the rivet has been set because it will be in the way of creating a smooth curve.

6 Snap the compression rivets into place in the center hole of the disc, mounting a disc on each end of the bracelet cuff. They will be loose until you set them in the next step, so turn the discs so that the text on each faces the gap in the top of the cuff.

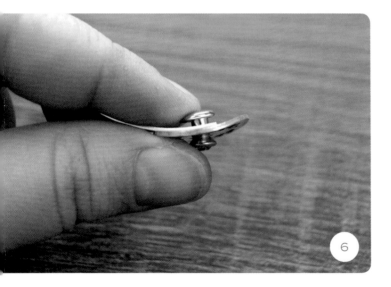

7 Finally, place the rivet, crystal side down, on a rubber block. Use the curved end of the rivet-setting tool, and place it over the curved back side of the crystal rivet. Tap the top of the tool several times with your hammer. The rubber block will absorb enough of the force that your crystal shouldn't crack, but this also means you may have to work harder at setting the rivet securely than when setting standard compression rivets, and may have to strike the rivet-setting tool a dozen times or more before the rivet is fully set. Test the security of the rivet by testing whether you can twist the charm at the end of the cuff; once it no longer moves, you can move on to the other side and repeat the process to finish the cuff. This twin charm cuff is an eye-catching piece with just enough sparkle to work with any super star's super style! ●

CHAPTER 5

Rings and Earrings

Rings and earrings may not immediately spring to mind when you think about stamped metal jewelry, but any blank metal surface is an opportunity to add a message or your favorite design! In this chapter, you'll explore ideas beyond necklaces and bracelets to get your creative juices flowing. The projects here range from simple beginner projects with single impressions, like the Dragonfly Charm Earrings, to rings that tell a story, like the Rings for Every Mood. Go for a big impact on a night out by making the Diva Chandelier Earrings, or try something understated and unique for everyday wear with the Free-Form Beaded Earrings. There's lots of room in this final chapter to make these styles all your own!

Rings for
Every Mood

HAND-STAMPED METAL JEWELRY is all about expressing yourself, and with this easy ring you can stamp a ring for every mood. Whether you're feeling goofy, sassy, nerdy, cranky, or something else entirely, you can tell the world without saying a word. These rings are also adjustable, so they're an easy gift to give without knowing someone's ring size! We'll make the "All Hail" Princess Ring here, but this tutorial is perfect for customization to make any ring you like.

materials

- 1 (½" × 2¼") aluminum ring blank
- Steel block
- Stamp Straight Tape or washi tape
- 6mm crown design stamp, or 6mm design stamp of your choice
- Stamping hammer
- Pen or fine-tip marker
- 2.5mm ImpressArt Scarlett's Signature font alphabet stamps, or 2.5mm alphabet stamps in font of your choice, in uppercase
- Awl
- Stamp enamel
- Paper towel
- Ring bending pliers
- Ring mandrel
- Nylon hammer

1. Adhere your aluminum ring blank to your steel block with Stamp Straight Tape, placing it where the bottom of the crown will be placed on the top line. Stamp the crown design, then remove the tape. Move the Stamp Straight Tape down to the second line, and use your pen or fine-tip marker to mark the placement of the seven-letter message on the tape. Stamp the words "ALL HAIL" and remove the tape again. Add a little more design to your ring by using your awl to create a semicircle of dots between the crown and the message below. This will fill empty space and add detail to your ring.

2. Apply the enamel by squirting a few lines directly onto your piece. Rub in the enamel with a paper towel, making sure it gets all the way into your impressions; wait 10 seconds, then polish it clean. Continue to wipe the piece gently until the surface is cleaned of any enamel, and all that remains are the darkened impressions. If you find that you've accidentally wiped it out of the impressions, you can re-apply it and try again. If this happens, try waiting a few seconds longer the second time before wiping the enamel away.

3. Begin forming your ring by squeezing it between ring bending pliers. This will not give you a perfect rounded shape, but all you need to accomplish with the pliers is to form enough of a circle that you can slip the ring onto the ring mandrel.

4 To finish your ring and smooth the circle, use the nylon hammer to hammer the stamped blank as it rests around the ring mandrel—and you can even ensure the size is right during this step, by checking the size marks on the mandrel. As you hammer, the ring will tend to get larger, so occasionally you may need to pinch the two ends together to adjust it smaller, and move it up the mandrel until you've hammered it to a perfectly round shape. ●

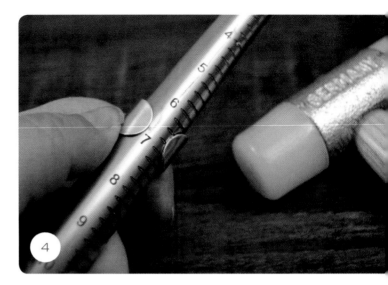

#happystamping

I used ImpressArt's 2.5mm Scarlett's Signature font, crown design stamp, pineapple design stamp, and paisley pattern stamp—but as long as the message is short, you can stamp anything you love on a ring blank.

Dragonfly Charm Earrings

DIY STAMPED METAL JEWELRY

DRAGONFLIES ARE SPECIAL to me because they remind me of my favorite lake and all the wonderful memories made there. Do you have special memories that a certain symbol brings back? Maybe a nickname you used to go by, a place close to your heart, or a sport that your sweetheart used to play? In a few simple steps, you can create these simple charm earrings with your favorite design stamp to match any outfit and bring back happy memories every time you wear them!

materials

- 2 (½") round aluminum tags
- Steel block
- Stamp Straight Tape or washi tape
- 6mm dragonfly design stamp
- Stamping hammer
- Stamp enamel
- Paper towel
- 2 (4mm) crystal beads
- 2 (2") silver finish jewelry eye pins
- Round nose pliers
- Wire cutters
- Chain nose pliers
- 2 (14mm) silver finish fishhook earring wires

1   Adhere your tag to your steel block with Stamp Straight Tape over the top ring of the blank. Center the dragonfly stamp on the blank, with the head at the ring end of the tag. Strike the stamp harder than you would for letter stamps; when working with large or detailed design stamps, more force is required to get a crisp impression. You must also be sure that your stamp is perfectly flat on the surface of your blank. Once you've completed your first charm, repeat this process for the second identical charm.

2   Apply the enamel to each blank by squirting a few lines directly onto each piece. Rub in the enamel with a paper towel, making sure it gets all the way into your impressions; wait 10 seconds, then polish it clean. Continue to wipe the piece gently until the surface is cleaned of any enamel, and all that remains are the darkened impressions. If you find that you've accidentally wiped it out of the impressions, you can re-apply it and try again. If this happens, try waiting a few seconds longer the second time before wiping the enamel away. Once you complete the first charm, repeat the darkening process for the second.

3 The next step is to create a beaded connector to add a bit of sparkle and color to your earrings. To do this, add a bead to a 2" eye pin. Grip the pin with your round nose pliers just above the bead on the wire end of the pin, and wrap the top of the pin around one side of your pliers, forming a loop. Create this loop oriented at a 90° angle from the loop at the opposite end of the pin to avoid adding unnecessary jump rings to your design.

4 Use your wire cutters to cut away the excess wire, so that the loop closes snugly at the top of the bead.

5 Finally, twist the loops of the connector open with your chain nose pliers to add the charm on one side and the earring wire on the other—just as you would do for a jump ring. Repeat the assembly to complete the pair, and these simple earrings will become a staple in your wardrobe! ●

#stampinghacks

If you find when you complete the assembly of your earrings that the charms face outward to the sides, rather than facing forward, you can easily correct the orientation by re-opening the loops and adding 4mm silver jump rings. Each jump ring you add to a design will rotate the components beneath it by 90°.

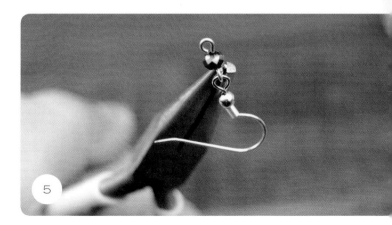

Aim High, Aim True
Earrings

DIY STAMPED METAL JEWELRY

IF YOU AIM high and aim true, you can achieve more than you think! Stamping blanks are being made in more shapes, sizes, and metals than ever before. These arrow earrings are part of a new trend coming on the stamping scene of artisan blanks that are beautiful on their own—and also customizable with your favorite message. These arrow blanks from Beaducation are a design that needs little embellishment, and you can find new styles and designs being released all the time from major stamping supply brands and independent artists alike.

materials

- 2 (43mm) Beaducation Pewter Arrow blanks
- Steel block
- 3mm ImpressArt Newsprint font alphabet stamps, or 3mm alphabet stamps in font of your choice, in uppercase
- Stamping hammer
- Stamp enamel
- Paper towel
- 4 (4mm) jump rings
- Chain nose pliers
- 2 (14mm) silver finish fishhook earring wires

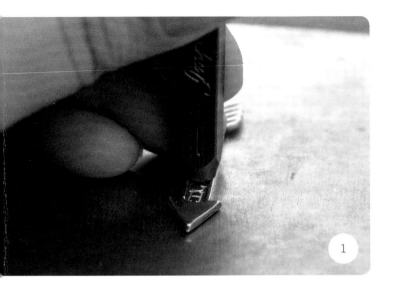

1 Place your blanks on your steel block. Placing each letter stamp between the two side channels of the blanks, stamp the first blank with the words "AIM HIGH" and the second with the words "AIM TRUE."

2 Apply the enamel to each arrow by squirting a few lines directly onto each piece. Rub in the enamel with a paper towel, making sure it gets all the way into your impressions; wait 10 seconds, then polish it clean. Continue to wipe the piece gently until the surface is cleaned of any enamel, and all that remains are the darkened impressions. If you find that you've accidentally wiped it out of the impressions, you can re-apply it and try again. If this happens, try waiting a few seconds longer the second time before wiping the enamel away. Darken one arrow first, and then repeat the process for the second arrow.

3 Add a little more texture around the arrowhead to give the impression that it was chipped away from stone by hammering the edges with the round end of your hammer.

DIY STAMPED METAL JEWELRY

4 Turn your arrow charms into earrings by connecting two jump rings to each arrow. Twist open a 4mm jump ring with your chain nose pliers by using two sets of pliers to grab on either side of the seam in the ring. Twist the pliers and ends of the jump ring away from each other in a north-south motion. Slide the stamped metal blank onto the jump ring, then close the ring by twisting the ends back toward each other so the ends of the ring are flush. Open a second ring (so that your earrings are aligned to face forward), add the earring wire and the attached jump ring, and twist it closed. Complete the pair by repeating the process with the other arrow, and make a statement that you've got your eyes on the prize! ●

#stampinghacks

You may have noticed I didn't use Stamp Straight Tape for the stamping in this project! If you feel confident in your stamping, try going tape-free! You can simply line up each letter below the one above it as you stamp your word down vertically.

Winter Weather
Stud Earrings

materials

THESE UNDERSTATED WINTER studs are simple and subtle, and you can make a new pair for any occasion! The all-over snowflake pattern is great for beginners, because you can easily hide any mistakes you make as you practice your strike among the flurry of stamps. Don't forget, if winter is still months away, you can modify this design with flowers, seashells, leaves, and more, giving you simple style for any season.

- 2 (½") aluminum circles
- Steel block
- Stamp Straight Tape or washi tape
- 6mm snowflake design stamp
- 3mm snowflake design stamp
- Stamping hammer
- Stamp enamel
- Paper towel
- Heavy-duty adhesive (like E6000)
- 2 (6mm) flat-backed earring studs

1. Begin by taping your aluminum disc to your steel block, to prevent it from slipping as you stamp. The placement of the tape doesn't matter, as you can move it around and replace it as you work, so that you can evenly cover the entire disc. Begin with your 6mm snowflake stamp, and stamp snowflakes onto the blank, covering it. Strike the top of the stamp with more force than you would use for letters, and check your results as you go. Stamp over the edges in some places, and don't forget to rotate and turn your stamp as you go so that you have snowflakes from every direction. When you've filled the blank with the large stamp, go back over the blank with the 3mm snowflake stamp, filling in the small spaces.

2. Apply the enamel by squirting a few lines directly onto your piece. Rub in the enamel with a paper towel, making sure it gets all the way into your impressions; wait 10 seconds, then polish it clean. Continue to wipe the piece gently until the surface is cleaned of any enamel, and all that remains are the darkened impressions. If you find that you've accidentally wiped it out of the impressions, you can re-apply it and try again. If this happens, try waiting a few seconds longer the second time before wiping the enamel away. Darken one disc first, and then complete the process for the second disc.

3 Hammer the edges of the discs with the round end of your hammer to give them a more finished look. It will also add a hint of shine to your studs, as the hammered edges will catch the light from different angles as you wear them.

4 Using a small dot of heavy-duty adhesive, glue the flat-backed studs to the back side of your stamped discs. Place the stud along the edge of the disc without going over the edge; you don't want the earring back to be visible from the front of the earrings. Because this is an all-over design, it doesn't matter which edge the backs are glued to; there's no right or wrong side up. Allow the glue to set for at least an hour until the glue holds the earring posts securely (or per the package instructions, which will vary by formula) and your wintry earrings are ready for any party! ●

#stampinghacks

If you find that your impression is too light, then use more force for the next strike. If you get a partial impression, then straighten your stamp and be sure it's level against the disc.

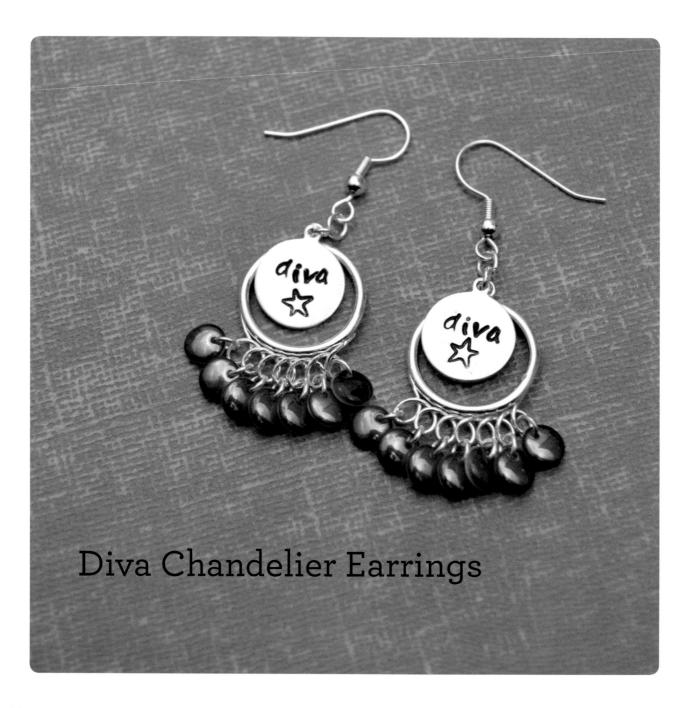

Diva Chandelier Earrings

materials

EVERY DIVA NEEDS great accessories, and personalized accessories are even better! These chandelier earrings are a great addition to your night-out jewelry, with just enough shine to get people's attention, but not so heavy that they become uncomfortable before the evening is out.

- 2 (½") round aluminum tags
- Steel block
- Stamp Straight Tape or washi tape
- Pen or fine-tip marker
- 2.5mm ImpressArt Scarlett Signature font alphabet stamps, or 2.5–3mm alphabet stamps in font of your choice, in lowercase
- 3mm star stamp
- Stamping hammer
- Stamp enamel

- Paper towel
- 2 (1") round silver finish chandelier earring bases, with 1 hole at the top and 7 at the bottom
- 18 (4mm) silver finish jump rings
- Chain nose pliers
- 14 (6mm) blue 1-hole lentil-shaped beads
- 2 (14mm) silver finish fishhook earring wires

1 Adhere your blanks to your steel block with Stamp Straight Tape, placing them with the ring end at the top of the disc. Position the top of the tape centered vertically on the circle, where the bottom of each letter will be stamped across the blank. Then use your pen or fine-tip marker to mark off the placement of your four letters to spell out the word "diva." Stamp your word and then use your star stamp to add a star imprint centered beneath the word. Once you've completed the first tag, repeat these steps to make a second identical tag.

2 Apply the enamel to each tag by squirting a few lines directly onto each piece. Rub in the enamel with a paper towel, making sure it gets all the way into your impressions; wait 10 seconds, then polish it clean. Continue to wipe the piece gently until the surface is cleaned of any enamel, and all that remains are the darkened impressions. If you find that you've accidentally wiped it out of the impressions, you can re-apply it and try again. If this happens, try waiting a few seconds longer the second time before wiping the enamel away. Darken one tag first, and then repeat the process for the second.

3   This base has 7 loops at the bottom, so you will need to open 7 jump rings, add beads, and connect each to a bottom loop. Do this by twisting open each 4mm jump ring with your chain nose pliers by using two sets of pliers to grab on either side of the seam in the ring. Twist the pliers and ends of the jump rings away from each other in a north-south motion. Slide the jump ring onto the chandelier earring base, add a bead, then close the ring by twisting the ends back toward each other so the ends of the ring are flush. Repeat this process for the remaining 6 holes in this earring base and for the 7 holes on the second earring base. If your lentil beads are 2-sided, be sure that each bead faces the same direction.

4   Connect your stamped charm to the top loop of the earring base using a jump ring, in the same manner. For a forward-facing orientation as shown here, attach a second jump ring to the first and add the earring wire.

5   Complete the second earring and you'll be ready to hit the town with these shining earrings. If you don't consider yourself a diva, you can add any design stamp, initials, or a word that speaks to you instead! ●

Flower Garden
Wire-Wrapped Earrings

materials

THE ORGANIC LOOK of aged brass and the floral texture in these earrings reminds me of all things vintage, and the modern contrast between the wire and metal makes for a striking combination of old and new. If your style defies a category, then you'll want to try these simply designed earrings. You can also play it subtle if you prefer to match your wire to your brass blanks and allow the textures in this project to take center stage.

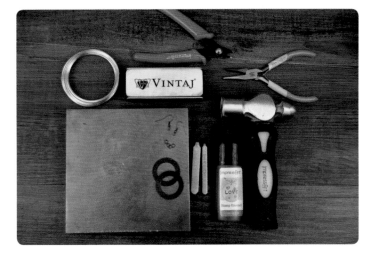

- Stamp Straight Tape or washi tape
- 2 (25mm) brass washer blanks, treated with patina
- Steel block
- 6mm flower design stamp
- 3mm flower design stamp
- Stamping hammer
- Buffing pad or buffing block
- Stamp enamel
- Paper towel
- Nylon hammer
- 48" (22-gauge) silver plated copper wire, cut into 2 (24") pieces
- Chain nose pliers
- Wire cutters
- 4 (4mm) brass finish jump rings
- 2 (14mm) brass finish fishhook earring wires

1 Tape your washer blanks to your steel block to hold them steady while you work, and stamp them all over with the 6mm flower design stamp, making sure to stamp over the edges and rotate your stamp as you work for a random, all-over pattern. At some point, you will need to move your tape so that you can cover the entirety of both blanks with flowers. When you have filled the washers with large flowers, use your 3mm flower stamp and fill in the small areas between. Gently buff the stamped discs with the buffing pad or buffing block to bring a little shine back, and to add some light contrast to the flowers.

2 Apply the enamel by squirting a few lines directly onto your piece. Rub in the enamel with a paper towel, making sure it gets all the way into your impressions; wait 10 seconds, then polish it clean. Continue to wipe the piece gently until the surface is cleaned of any enamel, and all that remains are the darkened impressions. If you find that you've accidentally wiped it out of the impressions, you can re-apply it and try again. If this happens, try waiting a few seconds longer the second time before wiping the enamel away. Darken one washer first, then complete the step for the second washer.

3 Thin blanks tend to curl the more you stamp on the front side, so you may also need to flatten the blank back out with your nylon hammer after stamping. Simply turn the blank face down on your steel block, and hammer the back side until it's flat again.

#happystamping

Make these earrings uniquely you by making changes to the metals and design themes you choose!

DIY STAMPED METAL JEWELRY

4   Position the bend of your folded wire at the bottom point of your washer at the point opposite from the top hole, and begin wrapping around the bottom edge of the washer with one end of the wire either to the right or to the left. When wrapping wire, you want to get your coils as close as possible to each other. When you run out of wire, do your best to tuck it behind the neighboring coil to prevent getting accidentally scratched later. If your wire runs out at the front side of your washer, trim it down slightly with your wire cutters so that the end is to the back. Use your chain nose pliers to crease the final coil, ensuring that the wire stays in place.

5   Attach a 4mm jump ring to the top of your washer by twisting open the jump ring with your chain nose pliers by using two sets of pliers to grab on either side of the seam in the ring. Twist the pliers and ends of the jump ring away from each other in a north-south motion. Slide the ring onto the washer, then close the ring by twisting the ends back toward each other so the ends of the ring are flush. For washers that face forward when you wear them as shown here, add an additional jump ring to the previous ring when attaching the earring wires. If you prefer a side-facing design, omit the second ring. Repeat this step for the second washer, completing your pair of earrings. ●

Free-Form Beaded Earrings

IF YOU'RE MORE of a free spirit when it comes to accessories, I have one final design to share with you that allows you to hammer and form wire into unique shapes, and add depth and texture to it with design stamps. This technique can be applied to more than just earrings if you find you enjoy it! We're going out with a bang on this project—literally—while you give your hammers a workout making these free-form earrings.

materials

- 8–10" (14-gauge) silver plated copper wire
- Chasing hammer
- Stamp Straight Tape or washi tape
- Steel block
- 3mm spiral design stamp
- Stamping hammer
- Stamp enamel
- Paper towel
- 6 (size ⁶⁄₀) glass seed beads
- Round nose pliers
- Wire cutters
- 2 (4mm) jump rings
- Chain nose pliers
- 2 (14mm) silver finish fishhook earring wires

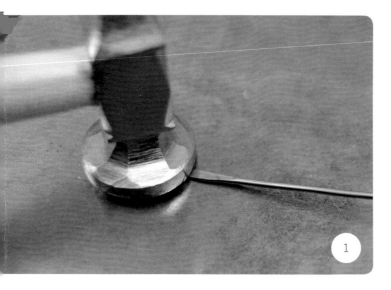

1 Cut your 14-gauge wire into 2 pieces, each 4" or 5" long. This is a longer length than you need, but forming wire is easier when you have more length to bend into shape. Using the flat face of your chasing hammer, strike the end of the wire until the bottom ½" to 1" of it flattens out to a 3–4mm width—a width similar to your design stamp. Leave the upper part of the wire rounded. Repeat with the second piece of wire. While hammering this second wire, do your best to match the hammered length of your first earring. While they don't need to look exactly alike, having them the same length is the only real goal.

2 Tape the segment of wire to your steel block, allowing the flattened area to rest against the steel. Stamp the flattened area with the spiral design stamp, beginning at the bottom and working toward the still-rounded wire, creating 3–4 impressions. Your flattened wire may not be quite as wide as your spiral stamp, and that's fine if the design goes over the edges. The goal here is simply to fill the flattened area with texture, unlike stamping a specific word. Repeat with the second length of flattened wire.

3 Apply the enamel by squirting a few lines directly onto your piece. Rub in the enamel with a paper towel, making sure it gets all the way into your impressions; wait 10 seconds, then polish it clean.

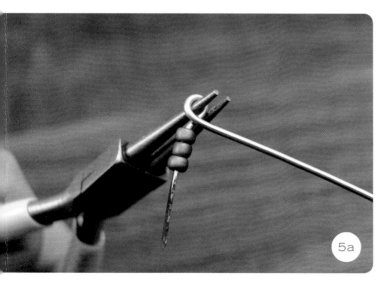

DIY STAMPED METAL JEWELRY

4   Continue to wipe the piece gently until the surface is cleaned of any enamel, and all that remains are the darkened impressions. If you find that you've accidentally wiped it out of the impressions, you can re-apply it and try again. If this happens, try waiting a few seconds longer the second time before wiping the enamel away. Darken the impressions on one piece first, then repeat this step for the second piece.

5   Add three large seed beads onto the rounded end of the wire. The flattened area will be wide enough to act as a stopper for the beads, holding them in place. Then grip the wire with your round nose pliers just above the beads on the rounded part of the wire, and bend it backward (away from your stamped design), forming a loop with the wire. Cut off the excess wire with your wire cutters at the bottom of the loop. The wire will be slightly off-center, so simply push it into place with your pliers so that the loop is closed. Repeat this step on the second piece of wire to make your second earring.

6   Twist open a 4mm jump ring with your chain nose pliers by using two sets of pliers to grab on either side of the seam in the ring. Twist the pliers and ends of the jump ring away from each other in a north-south motion. Slide the bead loop and earring wire onto the jump ring, then close the ring by twisting the ends back toward each other so the ends of the ring are flush. Repeat with the second bead and earring wire. Wear your Free-Form Beaded Earrings with a free-spirit attitude! ●

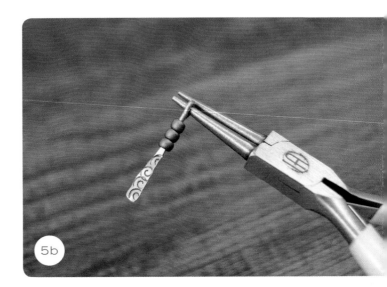

5b

appendix

U.S./METRIC CONVERSION CHART

U.S. Length Measure	Metric Equivalent
¼ inch	0.6 centimeters
½ inch	1.2 centimeters
¾ inch	1.9 centimeters
1 inch	2.5 centimeters
1½ inches	3.8 centimeters
1 foot	0.3 meters
1 yard	0.9 meters

index

Page Numbers in *italics* indicate projects. Page numbers in **bold** indicate tutorial projects.

about the author

ADRIANNE SURIAN lives in beautiful Grand Rapids, Michigan, and is totally into instant-gratification and all things DIY. When she's not chasing her kids around making sure they're fed and clothed, she is an artist, craft project designer, and author. Her work has been featured in multiple art exhibits, and she loves mixing media using metals, glass, and other elements in unusual ways. She shares craft projects, DIY accessories, and home decor on her website, Happy Hour Projects, and for other national brands and retailers.

That's right, *she's got crafty street cred* (that's totally a thing). She loves to make pretty things and share them with awesome people! She carves out a little time nearly every day for creativity—hour-or-less projects are her specialty, so it fits the crazy schedule of being a mother and a responsible bill-paying adult. In that hour each day, she crafts and balances new cocktails, hammers on metal, cuts, paints, glues, and glazes. Then after her kiddos go to bed, she spends quality time writing until the wee hours of the morning, all out of an enthusiasm for making something with her own two hands, then sitting down to teach it to people just like you.

You can find Adrianne online here:

- Her Blog: http://happyhourprojects.com
- Facebook: www.facebook.com/happyhourprojects
- Instagram: www.instagram.com/HappyHrProjects
- Pinterest: www.pinterest.com/happyhrprojects
- Twitter: https://twitter.com/HappyHrProjects
- YouTube: www.youtube.com/adriannesurian